Good Housekeeping

easy to make!
Puddings & Desserts

COLLINS & BROWN

This edition published in Great Britain in 2011
by Collins & Brown
10 Southcombe Street
London W14 0RA

An imprint of Anova Books Company Ltd

The Good Housekeeping website is
www.allaboutyou.com/goodhousekeeping

10 9 8 7 6 5 4 3 2 1

ISBN 978-1-84340-648-8

A catalogue record for this book is available from
the British Library.

Reproduction by Dot Gradations Ltd
Printed and bound by Times Offset (M) Sdn. Bhd, Malaysia

This book can be ordered direct from the publisher at
www.anovabooks.com

NOTES

- Both metric and imperial measures are given for the recipes. Follow either set of measures, not a mixture of both, as they are not interchangeable.
- All spoon measures are level.
  1 tsp = 5ml spoon; 1 tbsp = 15ml spoon.
- Ovens and grills must be preheated to the specified temperature.
- Use sea salt and freshly ground black pepper unless otherwise suggested.
- Fresh herbs should be used unless dried herbs are specified in a recipe.
- Medium eggs should be used except where otherwise specified. Free-range eggs are recommended.
- Note that certain recipes, including mayonnaise, lemon curd and some cold desserts, contain raw or lightly cooked eggs. The young, elderly, pregnant women and anyone with an immune-deficiency disease should avoid these, because of the slight risk of salmonella.
- Calorie, fat and carbohydrate counts per serving are provided for the recipes.
- If you are following a gluten- or dairy-free diet, check the labels on all pre-packaged food goods.
- Recipe serving suggestions do not take gluten- or dairy-free diets into account.

Picture credits
Photographers: Craig Robertson; Nicki Dowey (pages 33, 34, 35, 37, 39, 40, 43, 48, 52, 55, 58, 60, 64, 69, 73, 75, 76, 79, 80, 84, 88, 97, 99, 104, 112, 113, 116, 117, 118, 119, 122, 125, 126)
Stylist: Helen Trent
Home economist: Mari Mererid Williams

easy to make!
Puddings & Desserts

Contents

Foreword

Cooking, for me, is one of life's great pleasures. Not only is it necessary to fuel your body, but it exercises creativity, skill, social bonding and patience. The science behind the cooking also fascinates me, learning to understand how yeast works, or to grasp why certain flavours marry quite so well (in my mind) is to become a good cook.

I've often encountered people who claim not to be able to cook – they're just not interested or say they simply don't have time. My sister won't mind me saying that she was one of those who sat firmly in the camp of disinterested domestic goddess. But things change, she realised that my mother (an excellent cook) can't always be on hand to prepare steaming home-cooked meals and that she actually wanted to become a mother one day who was able to whip up good food for her own family. All it took was some good cook books (naturally, Good Housekeeping was present and accounted for) and some enthusiasm and sure enough she is now a kitchen wizard, creating such confections that even baffle me.

I've been lucky enough to have had a love for all things culinary since as long as I can remember. Baking rock-like chocolate cakes and misshapen biscuits was a right of passage that I protectively guard. I made my mistakes young, so have lost the fear of cookery mishaps. I think it's these mishaps that scare people, but when you realise that a mistake made once will seldom be repeated, then kitchen domination can start.

This Good Housekeeping Easy to Make! collection is filled with hundreds of tantalising recipes that have been triple tested (at least!) in our dedicated test kitchens. They have been developed to be easily achievable, delicious and guaranteed to work – taking the chance out of cooking.

I hope you enjoy this collection and that it inspires you to get cooking.

Meike.

Meike Beck
Cookery Editor
Good Housekeeping

0

The Basics

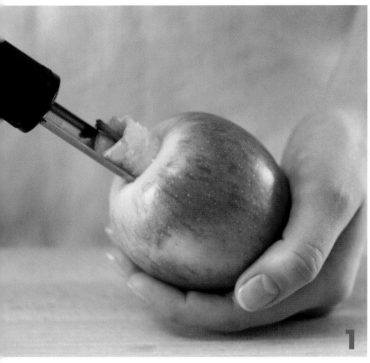

Preparing fruit

Fruit is a key element of many puddings and desserts, adding colour, taste and texture. Use in season for maximum flavour, either raw or cooked in a variety of different ways.

Preparing apples

1 **To core** an apple, push an apple corer straight through the apple from the stem to the base. Remove the core and use a small sharp knife to pick out any stray seeds or seed casings.

2 **To peel**, hold the fruit in one hand and run a swivel peeler under the skin, starting from the stem end and moving around the fruit, taking off the skin until you reach the base.

3 **To slice**, halve the cored apple. For crescent-shaped slices, stand the fruit on end and cut slices into the hollow as if you were slicing a pie. For flat slices, hold the apple cut-side down and slice with the knife blade at right angles to the hollow left by the core.

Preparing pears

1 **To core**, use a teaspoon to scoop out the seeds and core through the base of the pear. Trim away any remaining hard pieces with a small knife. If you halve or quarter the pear, remove any remaining seeds.

2 **To peel**, cut off the stem. Peel off the skin in even strips from tip to base.

3 **To slice**, halve the cored, peeled pear lengthways, then slice with the pear halves lying cut-side down on the board.

4 **To make pear fans**, slice at closely spaced intervals from the base to about 2.5cm (1in) from the tip, making sure you don't cut all the way through. Press gently to fan the slices, then use a palette knife to lift the pear gently on to your pie or plate.

Stoning larger fruit

Peaches, nectarines, plums, greengages and apricots can all be prepared in the same way.

1 Following the cleft along one side of the fruit, cut through to the stone all around the fruit.

2 Twist gently to separate the halves. Ease out the stone with a small knife. Rub the flesh with lemon juice to prevent discoloration.

Pitting cherries

A cherry stoner will remove the stones neatly, but it is important to position the fruit correctly.

1 First, remove the stems from the cherries, then wash the fruit and pat dry on kitchen paper. Put each cherry on the stoner with the stem end facing up. Close the stoner and gently press the handles together so that the metal rod pushes through the fruit, pressing out the stone.

2 Alternatively, if you do not have a cherry stoner, cut the cherries in half and remove the stones with the tip of a small pointed knife.

Preserving colour

The flesh of apples, pears and other fruit starts to turn brown when exposed to air. If you are not going to use the prepared fruit immediately, toss with lemon juice.

Peeling peaches

1 Peaches may be peeled for use in desserts. Put in a bowl of boiling water for 15 seconds to 1 minute (depending on ripeness). Don't leave in the water for too long, as the heat will soften the flesh. Put in a bowl of cold water.

2 Work a knife between the skin and flesh to loosen the skin, then gently pull to remove. Rub the flesh with lemon juice.

Stripping currants

Blackcurrants, redcurrants and whitecurrants can all be stripped quickly and simply from the stalk.

1 Run a fork a fork down the length of the stalk to strip off all the currants.

Washing berries

Most soft fruit can be washed very gently in cold water.

1 Put the berries in a bowl of cold water and allow any small pieces of dust or insects to float out.

2 Transfer the fruit to a colander and rinse gently under fresh running water. Drain well, then leave to drain on kitchen paper.

Hulling strawberries

1 Wash the strawberries with their stalks intact and dry on kitchen paper.

2 Remove the hull (the centre part that was attached to the plant) from the strawberry using a strawberry huller or a small sharp knife. Put the knife into the small, hard area beneath the green stalk and gently rotate to remove a small, cone-shaped piece.

Citrus fruit

Orange and lemon zest are important flavourings. Slices or segments of orange make a good dessert topping or decoration; they need to be prepared so that no skin, pith or membrane remains.

Zesting citrus fruit

Most citrus fruit is sprayed with wax and fungicides or pesticides. Unless you buy unwaxed fruit, wash it with a tiny drop of washing-up liquid and warm water, then rinse with clean water and dry thoroughly on kitchen paper.
To use a grater, rub the fruit over the grater, using a medium pressure to remove the zest without removing the white pith.
To use a zester, press the blade into the citrus skin and run it along the surface to take off long strips of zest.

Slicing

1 Cut off a slice at both ends of the fruit, then cut off the peel, just inside the white pith.

2 Gently hold the fruit on its side on the chopping board and use a serrated knife to cut slices no less than 5mm (¼ in) thick.

Segmenting

1 Cut off a slice at both ends of the fruit, then cut off the peel, just inside the white pith.

2 Hold the fruit over a bowl to catch the juice. Cut between the segments just inside the membrane to release the flesh. Continue until all the segments are removed. Squeeze the juice from the membrane into the bowl and use as required.

Pineapples

1 Cut off the base and crown of the pineapple, and stand the fruit on a chopping board. Using a medium-sized knife, peel away a section of skin, going just deep enough to remove all or most of the hard, inedible 'eyes'. Repeat all the way around.

2 Use a small knife to cut out any remaining traces of the eyes.

3 Cut the peeled pineapple into slices.

4 You can buy special tools for coring pineapples but a 7.5cm (3in) biscuit cutter works just as well. Put the pineapple slices on a board then place the cutter directly over the core and press down firmly to remove the core.

Mangoes

1 Cut a slice to one side of the stone in the centre. Repeat on the other side.

2 Cut parallel lines into the flesh of one slice, almost to the skin. Cut another set of lines to cut the flesh into squares.

3 Press on the skin side to turn the fruit inside out, so that the flesh is thrust outwards. Cut off the chunks close to the skin. Repeat with the other half.

Passion fruit

The seeds are edible, but if you want the fruit for a purée, you will need to sieve them.

1 Halve the passion fruit and scoop the seeds and pulp into a food processor or blender. Process for 30 seconds, until the mixture looks soupy. Or, scoop out the seeds and pulp into a sieve, as step 2.

2 Pour into a sieve over a bowl, and press down on the pulp with the back of a spoon to release the juice.

Papaya

To peel, use a swivel peeler, then cut in half lengthways. Use a teaspoon to scoop out the shiny black seeds and fibres inside the cavity.

Cooking fruit

Most fruit tastes marvellous raw and also makes superb desserts when poached or stewed, pan-fried or baked.

Poaching

Pears, apples and stone fruits are all well suited to gentle poaching in a sugar syrup. The secrets of successful poaching are never to let the liquid boil rapidly and never to overcook the fruit.

To serve four, you will need:
300g (11oz) sugar, 4 ripe pears, juice of 1 lemon.

1 Put the sugar in a large measuring jug and fill with cold water to make 1 litre (1¾ pints). Transfer to a pan and heat gently, stirring now and then, until the sugar dissolves.

2 Peel and halve the pears, and gently toss with the lemon juice.

3 Pour the sugar syrup into a wide-based pan and bring to a simmer. Put in the pears, cut sides down. They should be completely covered with syrup; add a little more syrup if necessary.

4 Simmer the fruit very gently for 30–40 minutes until tender when pierced with a knife or skewer. Serve hot, warm or chilled.

Stewing

To serve four, you will need:
450g (1lb) prepared fruit (chunks of apples and rhubarb, whole gooseberries, halved plums), 1 tbsp lemon juice, sugar (see Cook's Tips).

1 Put the fruit in a stainless steel pan with the lemon juice and sugar. Add 2 tbsp water. Bring to the boil over a medium heat, then turn down the heat and simmer gently, partly covered, until the fruit is soft, stirring often. Serve warm or chilled.

Cook's Tips

The type of fruit, its ripeness and your personal taste will dictate how much sugar is required. However, as a general rule:
• fruit that you can eat raw will need less sugar.
• fruit that you wouldn't eat raw such as rhubarb will need more sugar.

Baking

The key to success is to keep the cooking time short, so that the delicate flesh of the fruit doesn't break down completely.

1 Preheat the oven to 200°C (180°C fan oven) mark 6. Prepare the fruit and put in a single layer in a buttered baking dish or individual dishes. Put a splash of water in the dish(es). (For extra flavour, use fruit juice or wine instead.) Sprinkle with sugar (and other flavourings such as spices, citrus zest or vanilla, if you like). Dot with butter.

2 Bake the fruit until just tender when pierced with a knife or skewer: this should take 15–25 minutes depending on the fruit and the size of the pieces. Leave to stand for a few minutes before serving.

Grilling

Peaches, pineapples and bananas can be cooked under a hot grill.

1 Preheat the grill to high. Prepare the fruit and put in the grill pan (or a roasting tin) in a single layer. Sprinkle generously with sugar (and other flavourings such as ground cinnamon or ginger, if you like).

2 Set the grill pan under the grill about 10cm (4ir) from the heat. Grill until the top of the fruit is lightly caramelised and the fruit has softened, 5–8 minutes. Serve hot or warm.

Making fruit purée

Some fruits can be puréed raw, while others are better cooked. Leave cooked fruit to cool before puréeing.

1 Put a large spoonful of fruit in the blender and blend until smooth, then add another spoonful and blend again. Add the rest of the fruit in batches.

2 For a very smooth purée, pass the puréed fruit through a fine sieve, or use a mouli.

Pan-frying

Apples, pineapple, bananas and stone fruits such as peaches can be pan-fried to make a quick dessert.

To serve four, you will need:
450g (1lb) fruit, 25g (1oz) unsalted butter, 4 tbsp golden caster sugar, 1 tbsp lemon juice.

1 Prepare the fruit and cut into pieces no more than 2cm (³⁄₄ in) thick.

2 Melt the butter in a heavy-based frying pan and add the fruit. Stir to coat with butter, then cover and cook just long enough to heat through.

3 Uncover the pan and sprinkle on the sugar. Stir to coat well, and continue cooking, stirring regularly, until the fruit is soft but not mushy. Sprinkle with the lemon juice and toss just before serving.

Cracking and separating

Some recipes call for eggs to be separated into whites and yolks. It's easy, but it requires care. If you're separating more than one egg, break each one into an individual bowl or cup. Separating them individually means that if you break one yolk, you won't spoil the whole batch. Keeping the whites yolk-free is particularly important for techniques such as whisking.

1 Crack the egg sharply and carefully, right in the middle, to make a break between the two halves that is just wide enough to get your thumbnail into.

2 Holding the egg over a bowl with the ends downwards, carefully separate the halves. Some of the white will drip and slide into the bowl while the yolk sits in the end of the shell.

3 Carefully slide the yolk into the other end, then back again, to allow the remaining white to drop into the bowl. Take care not to break the yolk; even a speck can stop the whites from whisking up.

Preparing and using eggs

Eggs are a wonderfully versatile ingredient; they are used in a wide range of hot and cold desserts, from soufflés and meringues to pancakes and custards.

Pancakes

To make eight pancakes, you will need:
125g (4oz) plain flour, a pinch of salt, 1 medium egg, 300ml (1/2 pint) milk, oil and butter to fry.

1 Sift the flour and salt into a bowl, make a well in the centre and whisk in the egg. Gradually beat in the milk to make a smooth batter, then leave to stand for 20 minutes.

2 Heat a heavy-based frying pan and coat lightly with fat. Pour in a little batter and tilt the pan to coat the base thinly and evenly.

3 Cook over a moderately high heat for 1 minute or until golden. Turn carefully and cook the other side for 30 seconds to 1 minute.

Whisking

1 Use an electric mixer or wire whisk. Make sure that there is no trace of yolk in the whites and that the whisk and bowl are clean, completely grease-free and dry. At a low speed, use the whisk in a small area of the whites until they start to become foamy.

2 Increase the speed and work the whisk through the whites until soft peaks form. Do not over-whisk as the foam will become dry and grainy.

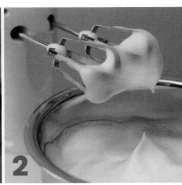

Meringues

Baking meringues is best done whenever you know you won't be needing your oven for a good few hours, as they must be left to dry in the turned-off oven for several hours or overnight.

To make 12 meringues, you will need:
3 medium egg whites, 175g (6oz) caster sugar.

1 Preheat the oven to 170°C (150°C fan oven) mark 3. Cover a baking sheet with baking parchment. Put the egg whites into a large, clean, grease-free bowl.

2 Whisk them until soft peaks form. Add a spoonful of sugar and whisk until glossy.

3 Keep adding the sugar a spoonful at a time, whisking thoroughly after each addition, until you have used half the sugar. The mixture should be thick and glossy.

4 Sprinkle the remaining sugar over the mixture and then gently fold in using a metal spoon.

5 Hold a dessertspoon in each hand and pick up a spoonful of mixture in one spoon, then scrape the other spoon against it to lift the mixture off. Repeat the process a few times, to form a rough oval shape. Using the empty spoon, push the oval on to the baking sheet; hold it just over the sheet so that it doesn't drop from a great height. Continue this process with the remaining mixture to make 12 meringues.

6 Put the meringues in the oven and bake for 15 minutes, then turn the oven off and leave them in the oven to dry out for several hours or overnight.

Working with sugar

Sugar is essential to many desserts. When heated it can be transformed entirely – into crisp caramel or delicate spun sugar.

Wet caramel

A good sauce to use with fruit such as oranges, peaches and pineapple.

1 Put 200g (7oz) caster sugar in a heavy-based pan with 150ml (¼ pint) water. Heat gently until the sugar dissolves. Turn up the heat and bring to the boil, then cook until it turns a medium caramel colour.

2 Remove the pan from the heat, stand well back and pour in 150ml (¼ pint) water. Heat and stir to dissolve, then cool.

Dry caramel

Use to make decorations. They can be made up to 24 hours in advance and stored in an airtight container.

1 Line a baking sheet with oiled greaseproof paper. Put 200g (7oz) caster sugar in a heavy-based pan with 4 tbsp water. Heat gently until the sugar dissolves.

2 Turn up the heat and bring to the boil, then cook until it turns a medium caramel colour. Dip the base of the pan in cold water. Use immediately, before the caramel begins to harden.

3 **For caramel flowers**, dip a fork into the caramel and, working quickly, make flower shapes about 4cm (1½ in) in diameter on oiled greaseproof paper.

4 **For caramel cages**, lightly oil the back of a ladle. Drizzle caramel threads over the ladle in a crisscross pattern, finishing with a thread around the rim.

Spun sugar

One of the most attractive sugar decorations, spun sugar is made from a light caramel syrup spun into a nest of hair-thin threads. You will need two forks, a rolling pin and sheets of paper to catch any drips of syrup that fall to the floor while you work.

1 Put 200g (7oz) caster sugar in a heavy-based pan with 4 tbsp water. Heat gently until the sugar dissolves.

2 Turn up the heat and bring to the boil. Continue to boil the syrup until it turns a light caramel colour. Dip the base of the pan in cold water, then leave to cool for 5 minutes.

3 Dip two forks, held in one hand, into the caramel. Flick them back and forth over a rolling pin held in your other hand, so that wispy threads fall over the pin.

4 When the rolling pin is full, carefully slide the threads off and gently form them into a ball or keep them as straight threads. Use immediately to decorate desserts.

Sugar syrup

Perfect for dressing up a fruit salad or drizzling over a sponge. Serve the syrup plain or add a flavouring (see Flavourings).

1 Put 275g (10oz) granulated sugar in a pan with 600ml (1 pint) cold water. Put the pan over a low heat and heat gently until the sugar has completely dissolved.

2 Bring the mixture to the boil and cook for 3 minutes.

3 Allow the syrup to cool. Use immediately or store in a jar in the refrigerator for up to one week.

Cook's Tips

When making caramel or spun sugar, watch the syrup closely once it starts to colour. The colour can deepen rapidly and very dark caramel tastes bitter.
Have a pan of cold water ready to dip the base of the pan in to stop the caramel cooking further.

Flavourings

Add the thinly pared zest of 1 lemon or $\frac{1}{2}$ orange to the sugar and water in step 1.
For a boozy sugar syrup, add 1–2 tbsp brandy or rum at the end of step 2.

Shaving

This is the easiest decoration of all because it doesn't call for melting the chocolate.

1 Hold a chocolate bar upright on the worksurface and shave pieces off the edge with a swivel peeler.

2 Alternatively, grate the chocolate against a coarse or medium-coarse grater to make very fine shavings.

Using chocolate

Chocolate is a delicious dessert ingredient. It also makes great decorations, and a simple sauce with many variations.

Melting

For cooking or making decorations, chocolate is usually melted first.

1 Break the chocolate into pieces and put in a heatproof bowl or in the top of a double boiler. Set over a pan of gently simmering water.

2 Heat very gently until the chocolate starts to melt, then stir only once or twice until completely melted.

Cook's Tips

- -

When melting chocolate, use a gentle heat.
Don't let water or steam touch the chocolate or it will 'seize' – become hard and unworkable. If it has seized, you can try to save it by stirring in a few drops of flavourless vegetable oil.

Chocolate curls

1 Melt the chocolate and spread it in a thin layer on a marble slab or clean worksurface. Leave to firm up.

2 Use a sharp blade (such as a pastry scraper, a cook's knife or a very stiff spatula) to scrape through the chocolate at a 45-degree angle. The size of the curls will be determined by the width of the blade.

Chocolate sauce

1 Chop plain chocolate (at least 70% cocoa solids) and put it in a saucepan with 50ml (2fl oz) water per 100g (3½oz) chocolate.

2 Heat slowly, allowing the chocolate to melt, then stir until the sauce is smooth. To liven up this simple chocolate sauce, see the Variations below.

Variations

These are all suitable for a sauce made with 200g (7oz) chocolate:

Milk or single cream Substitute in whole or in part for the water.

Coffee Stir in a teaspoon of instant coffee or a shot of espresso when melting the chocolate.

Spices Add a pinch of ground cinnamon, crushed cardamom seeds or freshly grated nutmeg to the melting chocolate.

Vanilla Stir in ¼ tsp vanilla extract when melting the chocolate.

Rum, whisky or cognac Stir in about 1 tsp alcohol when melting the chocolate.

Butter Stir in 25g (1oz) towards the end of heating.

Which chocolate to choose?

The type of chocolate you choose will have a dramatic effect on the end product. For the best results, buy chocolate that has a high proportion of cocoa solids, preferably at least 70%.

Blanching and skinning

After nuts have been shelled, they are still coated with a skin, which, although edible, tastes bitter. This is easier to remove if the nuts are blanched.

1 Put the shelled nuts in a bowl and cover with boiling water. Leave for 2 minutes, then drain.

2 Remove the skins by rubbing the nuts in a teatowel or squeezing between your thumb and index finger.

Toasting

Toasting improves the flavour of many nuts; if you toast nuts in their skins, the skins will rub off easily after toasting.

1 Preheat the oven to 200°C (180°C fan oven) mark 6. Put the shelled nuts on a baking sheet in a single layer and bake for 8–15 minutes until the skins are lightly coloured.

2 Remove the skins by rubbing the nuts in a teatowel.

Preparing and using nuts

Nuts feature in many desserts and puddings. Some can be bought ready-prepared, but here are various tips and techniques that may be helpful.

Chopping

Only chop about 75g (3oz) of nuts at a time. Unless you want very large pieces, the easiest way to chop nuts is in the food processor. Store chopped nuts in an airtight container for up to two weeks.
Note: Allow nuts to cool completely after skinning and before chopping.

1 Put the nuts in a food processor and pulse at 10-second intervals. Chop to the size of coarse breadcrumbs.

2 Alternatively, place a chopping board on a folded teatowel on the worksurface to give stability and use a cook's knife.

Slicing and slivering

Although you can buy sliced and slivered nuts, it's easy enough to make your own.

1 **To slice**, put the skinned nuts on a board. Using a cook's knife, slice the nuts as thinly as required.

2 **To make slivers**, carefully cut the slices to make narrow matchsticks.

Storing nuts

Because of their high fat content, nuts do not keep particularly well and turn rancid if kept for too long.
Always buy nuts from a shop with a high turnover of stock so you know they're likely to be fresh.
Store in an airtight container in a cool, dark place, or in the refrigerator, and use by the 'best before' date on the pack.

Nut Praline

Use crushed or ground to flavour ice creams and desserts.

To serve four, you will need:
250g (9oz) golden caster sugar, 175g (6oz) nuts.

1 Line a baking sheet with baking parchment and fill a bowl with very cold water. Put the sugar in a heavy-based pan over a low heat. Shake the pan gently to dissolve the sugar.

2 When the sugar has turned a dark golden brown, pour in the nuts and stir once with a wooden spoon.

3 Dip the base of the pan into cold water to prevent the praline from burning, then quickly pour the praline on to the parchment and spread out. Cool for 20 minutes, then break into pieces with a rolling pin. For fine praline, crush in a food processor or coffee grinder.

Making ice cream

Rich and creamy, fresh and fruity or sweet and indulgent, ice creams and iced desserts are easy to make. Good ice cream should have a smooth, creamy texture. Using an ice-cream maker is the best way to achieve it, but freezing and breaking up the ice crystals by hand works well, too.

Vanilla Ice Cream

To serve four to six, you will need:
300ml (½ pint) milk, 1 vanilla pod, split lengthways, 3 medium egg yolks, 75g (3oz) golden caster sugar, 300ml (½ pint) double cream.

1 Put the milk and vanilla in a pan. Heat slowly until almost boiling. Cool for 20 minutes, then remove the vanilla pod. In a large bowl, whisk the egg yolks and sugar until thick and creamy. Gradually whisk in the milk, then strain back into the pan.

2 Cook over a low heat, stirring with a wooden spoon, until thick enough to coat the back of the spoon – do not boil. Pour into a chilled bowl and leave to cool.

3 Whisk the cream into the custard. Pour into an ice-cream maker and freeze or churn according to the manufacturer's instructions or make by hand (see above right). Store in a covered freezerproof container for up to two months. Put the ice cream in the refrigerator for 15–20 minutes before serving to soften slightly.

Variations

Fruit Ice Cream: sweeten 300ml (½ pint) fruit purée (such as rhubarb, gooseberry, raspberry or strawberry) to taste, then stir into the cooked custard and churn.
Chocolate Ice Cream: omit the vanilla and add 125g (4oz) plain chocolate to the milk. Heat gently until melted, then bring almost to the boil and proceed as above.
Coffee Ice Cream: omit the vanilla and add 150ml (¼ pint) cooled strong coffee to the cooked custard.

Making ice cream by hand

1 If possible, set the freezer to fast-freeze 1 hour ahead. Pour the ice-cream mixture into a shallow freezerproof container, cover and freeze until partially frozen.

2 Spoon into a bowl and mash with a fork to break up the ice crystals. Return to the container and freeze for another 2 hours. Repeat and freeze for another 3 hours.

Layering

1 For a layered effect, make two or more flavoured ice creams of distinct colours. While the first ice cream is still soft, pack it into a mould lined with clingfilm. Freeze until firm, then layer the second ice cream on top and freeze until firm.

2 Continue in the same way with the remaining flavour(s). Serve cut into slices.

Ice cream bombes

1 Make two flavoured ice creams of distinct colours. While the first ice cream is still soft, press it against the sides and base of a large mould or bowl lined with clingfilm, making a hollow in the centre. Freeze until firm.

2 Fill the hollow with the soft second ice cream and cover with clingfilm. Freeze until firm, then unmould and serve in slices.

Rippling

1 Make vanilla ice cream and churn in an ice-cream maker (or make by hand) until thick, but soft. Spoon some of the ice cream into a bowl, or directly into a freezerproof container, then drizzle with fruit purée. Top with more ice cream and fruit purée.

2 Pass a wooden spoon handle through the ice cream five or six times to ripple the ice cream. Freeze for 4–5 hours until firm.

Vanilla Custard

To serve eight, you will need:
600ml (1 pint) full-fat milk, 1 vanilla pod or 1 tbsp vanilla extract, 6 large egg yolks, 2 tbsp golden caster sugar, 2 tbsp cornflour.

1 Put the milk in a pan. Split the vanilla pod and scrape the seeds into the pan, then drop in the pod. If using vanilla extract, pour it in. Bring to the boil, then turn off the heat and leave to cool for 5 minutes.

2 Put the egg yolks, sugar and cornflour in a bowl and whisk to blend. Remove the vanilla pod from the milk and gradually whisk the warm milk into the egg mixture.

3 Rinse out the pan. Pour the custard back in and heat gently, stirring constantly, for 2–3 minutes. The mixture should thicken enough to coat the back of a wooden spoon in a thin layer. Remove the pan from the heat.

Accompaniments

Perfect as an accompaniment to many desserts, a simple vanilla custard can be served hot or cold. Chilled fruit purées are great with ice cream and meringues.

Cook's Tip

Make custard up to four hours in advance. If you are not serving the custard immediately, pour it into a jug. Cover the surface with a round of wet greaseproof paper to prevent a skin from forming, then cover with clingfilm and chill. To serve hot, reheat very gently.

Raspberry Coulis

To serve four to six, you will need:
225g (8oz) raspberries, 2 tbsp Kirsch or framboise eau de vie (optional), icing sugar to taste.

1 Put the raspberries in a blender or food processor with the Kirsch or eau de vie, if using. Whiz until they are completely puréed.

2 Transfer the purée to a fine sieve, and press and scrape it through the sieve until nothing is left but the dry pips.

3 Sweeten with icing sugar to taste and chill until needed.

Variations

- -

Use different soft fruits and liqueurs. For example, try crème de cassis with blackcurrants or Amaretto with apricots.

Food storage and hygiene

Storing food properly and preparing it in a hygienic way is important to ensure that it remains as nutritious and flavourful as possible, and to reduce the risk of food poisoning.

Hygiene

When you are preparing food, always follow these important guidelines:

Wash your hands thoroughly before handling food and again between handling different types of food, such as eggs and cream. If you have any cuts or grazes on your hands, be sure to keep them covered with a waterproof plaster.

Wash down worksurfaces regularly with a mild detergent solution or multi-surface cleaner.

Use a dishwasher if available. Otherwise, wear rubber gloves for washing-up, so that the water temperature can be hotter than unprotected hands can bear. Change drying-up cloths and cleaning cloths regularly. Note that leaving dishes to drain is more hygienic than drying them with a teatowel.

Keep raw and cooked foods separate. Wash kitchen utensils in between preparing raw and cooked foods. Never put cooked or ready-to-eat foods directly on to a surface which has just had raw fish, meat or poultry on it.

Keep pets out of the kitchen if possible; or make sure they stay away from worksurfaces. Never allow animals on to worksurfaces.

Shopping

Always choose fresh ingredients in prime condition from stores and markets that have a regular turnover of stock to ensure you buy the freshest produce possible.

Make sure items are within their 'best before' or 'use by' date. (Foods with a longer shelf life have a 'best before' date; more perishable items have a 'use by' date.)

Pack frozen and chilled items in an insulated cool bag at the check-out and put them into the freezer or refrigerator as soon as you get home.

During warm weather in particular, buy perishable foods just before you return home. When packing items at the check-out, sort them according to where you will store them when you get home – the refrigerator, freezer, storecupboard, vegetable rack, fruit bowl, etc. This will make unpacking easier – and quicker.

The storecupboard

Although storecupboard ingredients will generally last a long time, correct storage is important:

Always check packaging for storage advice – even with familiar foods, because storage requirements may change if additives, sugar or salt have been reduced.

Check storecupboard foods for their 'best before' or 'use by' date and do not use them if the date has passed.

Keep all food cupboards scrupulously clean and make sure food containers and packets are properly sealed.

Once opened, treat canned foods as though fresh. Always transfer the contents to a clean container, cover and keep in the refrigerator. Similarly, jars, sauce bottles and cartons should be kept chilled after opening. (Check the label for safe storage times after opening.)

Transfer dry goods such as flour, sugar, rice and pasta to airtight, moisture-proof containers. When supplies are used up, wash the container well and dry thoroughly before refilling with new supplies.

Store oils in a dark cupboard away from any heat source as heat and light can make them turn rancid and affect their colour. For the same reason, buy olive oil in dark green bottles.

Store vinegars in a cool place; they can turn bad in a warm environment.

Store dried herbs, spices and flavourings in a cool dark cupboard or in dark jars. Buy in small quantities as their flavour will not last indefinitely.

Refrigerator storage

Fresh food needs to be kept in the cool temperature of the refrigerator to keep it in good condition and discourage the growth of harmful bacteria. Store day-to-day perishable items, such as opened jams, jellies and bottled sauces, in the refrigerator along with eggs and dairy products, fruit juices and salads. For pre-packed foods, always adhere to the 'use by' date on the packet.

A refrigerator should be kept at an operating temperature of 4–5°C. It is worth investing in a refrigerator thermometer to ensure the correct temperature is maintained.

To ensure your refrigerator is functioning effectively for safe food storage, follow these guidelines:

To avoid bacterial cross-contamination, store cooked and raw foods on separate shelves, putting cooked foods on the top shelf. Ensure that all items are well wrapped.

Never put hot food into the refrigerator, as this will cause the internal temperature of the refrigerator to rise.

Avoid overfilling the refrigerator, as this restricts the circulation of air and prevents the appliance from working properly.

It can take some time for the refrigerator to return to the correct operating temperature once the door has been opened, so don't leave it open any longer than is necessary.

Clean the refrigerator regularly, using a specially formulated germicidal refrigerator cleaner. Alternatively, use a weak solution of bicarbonate of soda: 1 tbsp to 1 litre (1³/₄ pints) water.

If your refrigerator doesn't have an automatic defrost facility, defrost regularly.

Maximum refrigerator storage times

The following storage times should apply, providing the food is in prime condition when it goes into the refrigerator and that your refrigerator is in good working order:

Fruit		Dairy Food	
Hard and stone fruit	3–7 days	Cheese, hard	1 week
		Cheese, soft	2–3 days
Soft fruit	1–2 days	Eggs	1 week
		Milk	4–5 days

Fruity Feasts

Oranges with Caramel Sauce

6 oranges
25g (1oz) butter
2 tbsp golden caster sugar
2 tbsp Grand Marnier
2 tbsp marmalade
grated zest and juice of 1 large orange
crème fraîche to serve

1 Preheat the oven to 200°C (180°C fan oven) mark 6. Cut away the peel and pith from the oranges, then put the oranges into a roasting tin just big enough to hold them.

2 Melt the butter in a pan and add the sugar, Grand Marnier, marmalade, orange zest and juice. Heat gently until the sugar dissolves.

3 Pour the sauce over the oranges, and bake in the oven for 30–40 minutes. Serve with crème fraîche.

Serves	EASY		NUTRITIONAL INFORMATION	
6	**Preparation Time** 15 minutes	**Cooking Time** 30-40 minutes	**Per Serving** 139 calories, 4g fat (of which 2g saturates), 24g carbohydrate, 0.1g salt	Vegetarian Gluten free

Try Something Different

- -

Use mango slices and blueberries and replace the Kirsch with Cointreau.

3 ripe peaches, halved, stoned and sliced
225g (8oz) wild strawberries or raspberries
3 tbsp Kirsch or eau de vie de Mirabelle
4 large egg yolks
50g (2oz) caster sugar

Summer Gratin

1 Put the peach slices in a bowl with the strawberries or raspberries and 2 tbsp Kirsch or eau de vie.

2 Put the egg yolks, sugar, remaining Kirsch and 2 tbsp water in a heatproof bowl over a pan of barely simmering water. Whisk for 5–10 minutes until the mixture leaves a trail and is warm in the centre. Remove from the heat. Preheat the grill.

3 Arrange the fruit in four shallow heatproof dishes and spoon the sauce over. Cook under the grill for 1–2 minutes or until light golden. Serve immediately.

EASY		NUTRITIONAL INFORMATION		Serves
Preparation Time 15 minutes	**Cooking Time** 15 minutes	**Per Serving** 168 calories, 4g fat (of which 1g saturates), 27g carbohydrate, 0g salt	Vegetarian Gluten free • Dairy free	**4**

Strawberry Compote

175g (6oz) raspberry conserve

juice of 1 orange

juice of 1 lemon

1 tsp rosewater

350g (12oz) strawberries, hulled and thickly sliced

150g (5oz) blueberries

1 Put the raspberry conserve in a pan with the orange and lemon juices. Add 150ml (¼ pint) boiling water. Stir over a low heat to melt the conserve, then leave to cool.

2 Stir in the rosewater and taste – you may want to add a squeeze more lemon juice if it's too sweet. Put the strawberries and blueberries into a serving bowl. Strain over the raspberry conserve mixture. Cover and chill overnight. Remove from the refrigerator about 30 minutes before serving.

Serves 4	EASY		NUTRITIONAL INFORMATION	
	Preparation Time 15 minutes, plus overnight chilling	**Cooking Time** 10 minutes	**Per Serving** 156 calories, trace fat, 40g carbohydrate, 0g salt	Vegetarian Gluten free • Dairy free

Try Something Different

Use a cinnamon stick instead of the star anise.

Spiced Nectarines

4 tbsp clear honey

2 star anise

1 tbsp lemon juice

4 ripe nectarines or peaches, halved and stoned

cream or vanilla ice cream to serve

1 Put the honey, star anise and lemon juice in a heatproof bowl. Stir in 150ml (¼ pint) boiling water and leave until just warm.

2 Add the nectarines to the warm honey syrup and leave to cool. Serve with cream or vanilla ice cream.

EASY		NUTRITIONAL INFORMATION		Serves
Preparation Time 10 minutes, plus cooling		**Per Serving** 95 calories, trace fat, 23g carbohydrate, 0g salt	Vegetarian Gluten free	4

Try Something Different

Use apricots instead of plums, and the seeds from
1 vanilla pod instead of the cardamom.

Plum and Cardamom Fool

1kg (2¼lb) dessert plums, stoned and sliced
125g (4oz) caster sugar
4 cardamom pods, split, seeds removed and crushed
2 tbsp lemon juice
150g (5oz) fresh custard
400g (14oz) Greek yogurt
amaretti biscuits to serve (optional)

1 Put the plums, sugar, cardamom seeds and lemon juice in a pan. Cover and bring to the boil. Simmer for 20–25 minutes until the plums are soft but still holding their shape. Pour into a cold bowl and leave for 30 minutes. Remove four slices for decoration and put to one side.

2 Strain the plums, reserving the juices. Purée the plums in a food processor and pour into a bowl. Boil the juices for 3–4 minutes until reduced to 3 tbsp, then stir into the plum purée with the custard and half the yogurt until smooth. Spoon into four glasses and chill for up to 2 hours. Decorate with the remaining yogurt and the reserved plum slices, and serve with amaretti biscuits if you like.

Serves 4	EASY		NUTRITIONAL INFORMATION	
	Preparation Time 15–20 minutes, plus standing and chilling	**Cooking Time** 30 minutes	**Per Serving** 365 calories, 11g fat (of which 5g saturates), 63g carbohydrate, 0.2g salt	Vegetarian Gluten free

4 Williams or Comice pears

150g (5oz) granulated sugar

300ml (½ pint) red wine

150ml (¼ pint) sloe gin

1 cinnamon stick

pared zest of 1 orange

6 star anise

Greek yogurt or whipped cream to serve (optional)

Drunken Pears

1 Peel the pears, cut out the calyx at the base of each and leave the stalks intact. Put the sugar, wine, sloe gin and 300ml (½ pint) water in a small pan and heat gently until the sugar dissolves.

2 Bring to the boil and add the cinnamon stick, orange zest and star anise. Add the pears, then cover and poach over a low heat for 30 minutes or until tender.

3 Using a slotted spoon, lift the pears into a bowl. Boil the liquid until it is syrupy and reduced to about 200ml (7fl oz). Pour over the pears and serve warm or chilled, with Greek yogurt or whipped cream if you like.

EASY		NUTRITIONAL INFORMATION		Serves
Preparation Time 15 minutes	**Cooking Time** about 40 minutes	**Per Serving** 305 calories, trace fat, 52g carbohydrate, 0g salt	Vegetarian Dairy free • Gluten free	**4**

Mango Gratin with Sabayon

3 large ripe mangoes, peeled, stoned and sliced
5 medium egg yolks
6 tbsp golden caster sugar
300ml (½ pint) champagne or sparkling wine
6 tbsp dark muscovado sugar to sprinkle
crisp sweet biscuits to serve

1 Arrange the mangoes in six serving glasses. Whisk the egg yolks and sugar in a large heatproof bowl over a pan of gently simmering water until the mixture is thick and falls in soft ribbon shapes. Add the champagne or sparkling wine and continue to whisk until the mixture is thick and foamy again. Remove from the heat.

2 Spoon the sabayon over the mangoes, sprinkle with the muscovado sugar, then blow-torch the top to caramelise or leave for 10 minutes to go fudgey. Serve with biscuits.

Serves	A LITTLE EFFORT		NUTRITIONAL INFORMATION	
6	**Preparation Time** 5 minutes, plus optional 10 minutes resting	**Cooking Time** 10 minutes	**Per Serving** 249 calories, 5g fat (of which 1g saturates), 45g carbohydrate, 0g salt	Vegetarian Gluten free • Dairy free

Spiced Winter Fruit

150ml (5fl oz) port

150ml (5fl oz) freshly squeezed orange juice

75g (3oz) light muscovado sugar

1 cinnamon stick

6 cardamom pods, lightly crushed

5cm (2in) piece fresh root ginger, peeled and thinly sliced

50g (2oz) large muscatel raisins or dried blueberries

1 small pineapple, peeled, cored and thinly sliced

1 mango, peeled, stoned and thickly sliced

3 tangerines, peeled and halved horizontally

3 fresh figs, halved

1 First, make the syrup. Pour the port and orange juice into a small pan, then add the sugar and 300ml (½ pint) cold water. Bring to the boil, stirring all the time. Add the cinnamon stick, cardamom pods and ginger, then bubble gently for 15 minutes.

2 Put all the fruit into a serving bowl. Remove the cinnamon stick and cardamom pods from the syrup – or leave in for a spicier flavour – then pour the syrup over the fruit. Serve warm or cold.

EASY		NUTRITIONAL INFORMATION		Serves
Preparation Time 20 minutes, plus cooling	**Cooking Time** 20 minutes	**Per Serving** 207 calories, trace fat, 45g carbohydrate, 0g salt	Vegetarian Gluten free • Dairy free	6

Fruity Fool

500g carton summer fruit compote
500g carton fresh custard

1 Divide half the compote among six serving glasses, then add a thin layer of custard. Repeat the process until all the compote and custard have been used.

2 Stir each fool once to swirl the custard and compote together, then serve.

Serves 6	EASY		NUTRITIONAL INFORMATION	
	Preparation Time 1-2 minutes		**Per Serving** 159 calories, 2g fat (of which trace saturates), 31g carbohydrate, 0.1g salt	Vegetarian Gluten free

Cook's Tip

To check whether a pineapple is ripe, pull on one of the leaves in the centre of the crown. If it pulls out easily, the fruit is ripe.

Caramelised Pineapple

1 large ripe pineapple, peeled and sliced into rounds
6 tbsp brown sugar
6 tbsp rum
2 tbsp olive oil

1 Cut each pineapple round in half and remove the core. Put the sugar and rum in a bowl with the pineapple and toss to coat.

2 Heat the oil in a non-stick frying pan until hot. Using a slotted spoon, lift the pineapple out of the bowl, keeping the liquid to one side, and fry over a medium heat for 4–5 minutes on each side until golden and caramelised.

3 Divide the pineapple among six plates. Add the rum and sugar to the pan and bubble for 1 minute. Drizzle over the pineapple to serve.

EASY		NUTRITIONAL INFORMATION		Serves
Preparation Time 10 minutes	**Cooking Time** about 20 minutes	**Per Serving** 187 calories, 4g fat (of which trace saturates), 31g carbohydrate, 0g salt	Vegetarian Gluten free • Dairy free	**6**

Baked Apricots with Caramelised Nuts

700g (1½lb) firm apricots
50g (2oz) butter
125g (4oz) caster sugar
100ml (3½fl oz) orange juice
vanilla ice cream to serve (optional)

For the caramelised nuts

75g (3oz) whole almonds, skinned
125g (4oz) caster sugar

1 Preheat the oven to 200°C (180°C fan oven) mark 6. Slit the apricots down one side (so they still look whole) and remove the stones. Put the apricots into an ovenproof dish. Gently melt the butter and sugar in a pan, stirring occasionally, until golden; remove from the heat. Carefully stir in the orange juice (it may splutter as the sugar hardens into lumps). Return the mixture to a low heat and stir until the sugar has dissolved; pour over the apricots.

2 Bake in the oven for 45 minutes or until the apricots are just soft, spooning the liquid over the fruit from time to time. Set aside and allow to cool. (Remove the skins at this stage if you like.)

3 Meanwhile, make the caramelised nuts. Put the almonds in a pan of cold water, bring to the boil and simmer for 2 minutes. Drain and cut the almonds into thick shreds (they will now be soft enough to chop without splintering). Put under a hot grill and toast until golden.

4 Put the sugar and 150ml (¼ pint) water in a pan, bring to the boil and bubble until the syrup turns a deep golden caramel. Take the pan off the heat and add 4 tbsp warm water. Return the pan to the heat and cook gently until the sugar has dissolved. Allow the mixture to cool, then stir in the almonds. Serve the apricots with scoops of vanilla ice cream if you like, with the caramelised nuts spooned over the top.

Cook's Tips

If the caramelised almond mixture sets, put back on the heat to warm slightly before spooning over the apricots.

To prepare ahead Complete the recipe to the end of step 3, then caramelise the nuts as in step 4. Spoon the almonds over the apricots, then cool, cover and chill for up to three days.

To use Warm the apricots and almonds in a shallow pan until the syrup melts. Complete the recipe.

To freeze Complete the recipe to the end of step 2, then cool, wrap and freeze.

To use Thaw the apricots for 4 hours or overnight at cool room temperature. Complete the recipe.

A LITTLE EFFORT		NUTRITIONAL INFORMATION		Serves
Preparation Time 20 minutes, plus cooling	**Cooking Time** 45–50 minutes	**Per Serving** 419 calories, 21g fat (of which 7g saturates), 55g carbohydrate, 0.2g salt	Vegetarian Gluten free	**4**

2

Cold and Chilled Desserts

Summer Pudding

800g (1lb 12oz) mixed summer berries,
such as 250g (9oz) each redcurrants and blackcurrants
and 300g (11oz) raspberries

125g (4oz) golden caster sugar

3 tbsp crème de cassis

9 thick slices of slightly stale white bread,
crusts removed

crème fraîche or cream to serve (optional)

1 Put the redcurrants and blackcurrants in a pan. Add the sugar and cassis. Bring to a simmer and cook for 3–5 minutes until the sugar has dissolved. Add the raspberries and cook for 2 minutes. Once the fruit is cooked, taste it – there should be a good balance between tart and sweet.

2 Meanwhile, line a 1 litre (1³/₄ pint) bowl with clingfilm. Put the base of the bowl on one piece of bread and cut around it. Put the circle of bread in the base of the bowl.

3 Line the inside of the bowl with more slices of bread, slightly overlapping to avoid any gaps. Spoon in the fruit, making sure the juice soaks into the bread. Keep back a few spoonfuls of juice in case the bread is unevenly soaked when you turn out the pudding.

4 Cut the remaining bread to fit the top of the pudding neatly, using a sharp knife to trim any excess bread from around the edges. Wrap in clingfilm, weigh down with a saucer and a tin can, and chill overnight.

5 To serve, unwrap the outer clingfilm, upturn the pudding on to a plate and remove the inner clingfilm. Drizzle over the reserved juice and serve with crème fraîche or cream if you like.

Serves 8	EASY		NUTRITIONAL INFORMATION	
	Preparation Time 10 minutes, plus overnight chilling	**Cooking Time** 10 minutes	**Per Serving** 173 calories, 1g fat (of which trace saturates), 38g carbohydrate, 0.4g salt	Vegetarian Dairy free

Try Something Different

Caribbean Crush: replace the sugar and liqueur with dulce de leche and the strawberries with sliced bananas.

200g (7oz) fromage frais, chilled

200g (7oz) low-fat Greek yogurt, chilled

1 tbsp golden caster sugar

2 tbsp strawberry liqueur

6 meringues, roughly crushed

350g (12oz) strawberries, hulled and halved

Eton Mess

1 Put the fromage frais and yogurt into a large bowl and stir to combine.

2 Add the sugar, strawberry liqueur, meringues and strawberries. Mix together gently and divide among six serving dishes.

EASY	NUTRITIONAL INFORMATION		Serves
Preparation Time 10 minutes	**Per Serving** 198 calories, 5g fat (of which 3g saturates), 33g carbohydrate, 0.1g salt	Vegetarian Gluten free	**6**

Lemon Meringue Pie

23cm (9in) ready-made sweet pastry case

For the filling

7 medium eggs, 4 separated, at room temperature

finely grated zest of 3 lemons

175ml (6fl oz) freshly squeezed lemon juice (about 4 lemons), strained

400g can condensed milk

150ml (¼ pint) double cream

225g (8oz) golden icing sugar

1 Preheat the oven to 180°C (160°C fan oven) mark 4. To make the filling, put 4 egg yolks in a bowl with the 3 whole eggs. Add the lemon zest and juice; whisk lightly. Mix in the condensed milk and cream.

2 Pour the filling into the pastry case and bake for 30 minutes or until just set in the centre. Set aside to cool while you prepare the meringue. Increase the oven temperature to 200°C (180°C fan oven) mark 6.

3 For the meringue, whisk the egg whites and icing sugar together in a heatproof bowl over a pan of gently simmering water, using a hand-held electric whisk, for 10 minutes or until very shiny and thick. Remove from the heat and continue to whisk at low speed for a further 5–10 minutes until the bowl is cool.

4 Pile the meringue on top of the lemon filling and swirl with a palette knife to form peaks. Bake for 5–10 minutes until the meringue is tinged brown. Leave to stand for about 1 hour, then serve.

Serves 8	EASY		NUTRITIONAL INFORMATION	
	Preparation Time 30 minutes	**Cooking Time** about 1 hour, plus 1 hour standing	**Per Serving** 692 calories, 36g fat (of which 21g saturates), 83g carbohydrate, 0.6g salt	Vegetarian

Try Something Different

Replace the mango with 300ml (¹/₂ pint) mixed berry purée and decorate with extra berries,

Mango and Lime Mousse

100ml (3¹/₂fl oz) double cream, plus extra to decorate

2 very ripe mangoes, peeled, stoned and sliced

finely grated zest and juice of 2 limes, plus zest of 1 lime to decorate

1 sachet powdered gelatine

3 large eggs, plus 2 yolks

50g (2oz) golden caster sugar

1 Whip the cream until just thick; chill. Purée the mango flesh in a blender to give 300ml (¹/₂ pint).

2 Put 3 tbsp of the lime juice in a small heatproof bowl, sprinkle the gelatine on top and leave to soak for 10 minutes.

3 In a large bowl, whisk together the eggs, extra yolks and sugar for 4–5 minutes until very thick and mousse-like. Very gently fold in the mango purée, whipped cream and lime zest.

4 Put the gelatine and lime mixture over a pan of boiling water for 1–2 minutes, stir until the gelatine dissolves, then lightly fold into the mango mixture until evenly combined. Divide among six glasses, freeze for 20 minutes, then transfer to the refrigerator to chill for at least 1 hour. To serve, decorate with whipped cream and lime zest.

EASY		NUTRITIONAL INFORMATION		Serves
Preparation Time 25–35 minutes, plus freezing and chilling	**Cooking Time** 1–2 minutes	**Per Serving** 209 calories, 14g fat (of which 7g saturates), 16g carbohydrate, 0.1g salt	Gluten free	**6**

Try Something Different

Use **raspberries or blueberries** instead of the strawberries.

Strawberry Brûlée

250g (9oz) strawberries, hulled and sliced
2 tsp golden icing sugar
1 vanilla pod
400g (14oz) Greek yogurt
100g (3½oz) golden caster sugar

1 Divide the strawberries among four ramekins and sprinkle with icing sugar.

2 Scrape the seeds from the vanilla pod and stir into the yogurt, then spread the mixture evenly over the fruit.

3 Preheat the grill to high. Sprinkle the caster sugar evenly over the yogurt until it's well covered.

4 Put the ramekins on a baking sheet or into the grill pan and grill until the sugar turns dark brown and caramelises. Leave for 15 minutes or until the caramel is cool enough to eat, or chill for up to 2 hours before serving.

Serves 4	EASY		NUTRITIONAL INFORMATION	
	Preparation Time 15 minutes, plus cooling and chilling	**Cooking Time** 5 minutes	**Per Serving** 240 calories, 10g fat (of which 5g saturates), 35g carbohydrate, 0.2g salt	Vegetarian Gluten free

Cook's Tips

Save 150 calories by replacing the double cream with whipping cream.
To prepare ahead Make the creams, but don't top with the berries and icing sugar. Chill for up to two days.
To use Complete the recipe, decorate with berries and icing sugar.

250g (9oz) raspberries

2 large eggs, plus 2 yolks

50g (2oz) caster sugar

300ml (½ pint) double cream

450g (1lb) mixed raspberries, strawberries and redcurrants to decorate

icing sugar to serve

Baked Raspberry Creams

1 Preheat the oven to 170°C (150°C fan oven) mark 3. Purée the raspberries in a food processor, then press through a sieve with the back of a spoon to remove the pips.

2 Whisk together the eggs, extra yolks and caster sugar. Strain into the puréed raspberries, pour in the cream and stir well.

3 Divide the mixture among six 150ml (¼ pint) ramekins, put in a roasting tin and pour enough water around the dishes to come halfway up the sides. Cover with oiled greaseproof paper and bake for 30–35 minutes until just set. Lift the dishes out of the roasting tin; cool, cover and chill overnight.

4 To serve, spoon the mixed fruit on top of the creams, and dust with icing sugar.

EASY		NUTRITIONAL INFORMATION		Serves
Preparation Time 15–20 minutes, plus overnight chilling	**Cooking Time** 30–35 minutes	**Per Serving** 347 calories. 30g fat (of which 17g saturates), 15g carbohydrate, 0.1g salt	Vegetarian Gluten free	6

Cook's Tip

Prepare the trifle up to the end of step 2 up to two days ahead. When ready to serve, complete the recipe. If you'd rather make the whole thing two days ahead, that's fine, but the cream will be firmer, rather than soft and luscious. Don't scatter over the toasted pecans until just before serving.

2 packs trifle sponges, each containing 8 sponges, or 1 ready-made Madeira cake – about 450g (1lb)

6 tbsp apricot jam

4 tbsp sherry

4 x 400g cans apricots in natural fruit juice, drained

2 x 400g cans peaches in natural fruit juice, drained

600ml (1 pint) double cream

500g carton fresh custard

250g (9oz) mascarpone

50g (2oz) pecan nuts, toasted

Apricot and Peach Trifle

1 Cut the trifle sponges in half horizontally, and spread one half with the apricot jam. Cover with the other half to make mini sandwiches. If using cake, cut into slices first, then sandwich together in pairs with jam. Use to line a large glass serving bowl. Drizzle over the sherry, then add the apricots.

2 Put the peaches in a food processor or blender, and whiz to a purée. Pour over the apricots.

3 Put the cream in a large bowl and whisk until soft peaks form. Chill. Put the whisk to one side – you needn't rinse it.

4 Put the custard and mascarpone in a large bowl and whisk together briefly to mix well. Pour over the fruit in an even layer.

5 Spoon the whipped cream over the custard mix and scatter the top with the toasted pecan nuts. Chill for at least 1 hour before serving.

Serves 10	EASY		NUTRITIONAL INFORMATION	
	Preparation Time 20 minutes, plus chilling		**Per Serving** 672 calories, 50g fat (of which 24g saturates), 49g carbohydrate, 0.4g salt	Vegetarian

Cook's Tips

Gelatine is available in leaf and powdered forms. Both must be soaked in liquid to soften before being dissolved in a warm liquid. Always add dissolved gelatine to a mixture that is warm or at room temperature – if added to a cold liquid, it will set in fine threads and spoil the final texture of the dish.

Gelatine is derived from meat bones, but there are vegetarian alternatives, such as agar agar and gelazone.

Elderflower and Fruit Jellies

2–3 tbsp elderflower cordial
200g (7oz) caster sugar
4 sheets leaf gelatine
150g (5oz) raspberries
150g (5oz) seedless grapes, halved

1 Put the elderflower cordial into a large pan and add 750ml (1¼ pints) water and the sugar. Heat gently, stirring until the sugar dissolves.

2 Put the gelatine in a bowl and cover with cold water. Leave to soak for 5 minutes. Lift out the softened gelatine, squeeze out the excess water, then add to the pan. Stir until dissolved, then strain into a large jug.

3 Divide the raspberries and grapes among six 200ml (7fl oz) glasses. Pour the liquid over the fruit, then cool and chill for at least 4 hours or overnight.

EASY		NUTRITIONAL INFORMATION		Serves
Preparation Time 15 minutes, plus minimum 4 hours chilling	**Cooking Time** 10 minutes	**Per Serving** 189 calories, trace fat, 42g carbohydrate, 0g salt	Gluten free Dairy free	**6**

Clementine and Cranberry Jellies

4 sheets leaf gelatine, snapped in half
600ml (1 pint) cranberry juice
2 tbsp golden caster sugar (optional)
8 clementines or mandarins, about 700g (1½lb)
150ml (¼ pint) single cream (optional)

1 Put the gelatine in a bowl and cover with cold water. Leave to soak for a few minutes until the gelatine softens. Meanwhile, put 150ml (½ pint) of the cranberry juice in a pan and add the sugar, if using. Gently bring to the boil, then remove from the heat.

2 Lift the softened gelatine out of the water and add to the heated cranberry juice. Stir until dissolved. Tip into a large jug and add the remaining cranberry juice. Set aside to cool, stirring occasionally so it doesn't set.

3 Pour some of the jelly into six 150ml (¼ pint) tall glasses, to come 2.5cm (1in) up the sides of each glass. Chill for 1 hour until set. Leave the remaining jelly out of the refrigerator.

4 Meanwhile, peel the clementines or mandarins, break the fruit into segments and remove as much of the white pith as possible.

5 Divide a third of the fruit among the glasses, packing the segments in tightly. Carefully pour over another layer of jelly so it just covers the fruit in each glass. Chill for 30 minutes until set. Repeat the layering and chilling process, finishing with a thin jelly layer.

6 Remove the set jellies from the refrigerator 15 minutes before serving, and flood the surfaces with a thin layer of single cream if you like.

Get Ahead

- -

To prepare ahead Complete the recipe to the end of step 5 up to two days ahead. Cover and chill.
To use Complete the recipe.

A LITTLE EFFORT		NUTRITIONAL INFORMATION		Serves
Preparation Time 30 minutes, plus cooling and 3–4 hours chilling	**Cooking Time** 5 minutes	**Per Serving** 152 calories, 5g fat (of which 3g saturates), 21g carbohydrate, 0g salt	Gluten free	**6**

Cook's Tip

Marinated Fruit: put 125ml (4fl oz) crème de cassis, the juice of 1 orange and 2 tbsp redcurrant jelly in a small pan. Heat gently to melt, then bubble for 2–3 minutes until syrupy. Pour into a large bowl to cool. Add 200g (7oz) raspberries and 4 nectarines, halved, stoned and sliced, and stir gently. Cover and chill. The flavour of the marinated fruit will be even better if you chill it overnight. (If the syrup thickens during chilling, stir in 1–2 tbsp orange juice.)

Almond Toffee Meringues

oil to grease

25g (1oz) light muscovado sugar

100g (3½oz) egg whites (about 3 medium eggs)

225g (8oz) caster sugar

25g (1oz) flaked almonds

Marinated Fruit (see Cook's Tip) and lightly whipped cream to serve

1 Preheat the oven to 170°C (150°C fan oven) mark 3 and preheat the grill. Lightly oil a baking sheet and sprinkle over the muscovado sugar. Grill for 2–3 minutes until the sugar begins to bubble and caramelise. Cool for about 15 minutes, then break the sugar into a food processor and whiz to a coarse powder.

2 Put the egg whites and caster sugar in a large, clean, grease-free bowl over a pan of gently simmering water: make sure the bowl does not touch the hot water. Stir until the sugar has dissolved and the egg white is warm, about 10 minutes.

3 Remove the bowl from the heat and place on a teatowel. Beat with an electric whisk for at least 15 minutes or until cold and glossy; the egg whites should stand in stiff shiny peaks when the whisk is lifted.

4 Cover two baking sheets with non-stick baking parchment. Fold half the powdered caramelised sugar into the meringue mixture. Spoon four oval mounds on to the baking sheets, leaving plenty of space between each. Sprinkle with flaked almonds and the remaining powdered sugar. Bake for 20 minutes, then turn off the heat and leave in the oven to dry out overnight. Serve with the Marinated Fruit and lightly whipped cream.

Serves	EASY		NUTRITIONAL INFORMATION	
4	**Preparation Time** 35 minutes, plus chilling	**Cooking Time** 22–25 minutes, plus overnight cooling	**Per Serving** 458 calories, 4g fat (of which trace saturates), 95g carbohydrate, 0.2g salt	Vegetarian Gluten free

Cook's Tip

Orange Poached Peaches: put 100g (3¹/₂oz) caster sugar in a pan with 600ml (1 pint) water and the grated zest and juice of 2 oranges. Bring to the boil and bubble for 5 minutes. Add 10 ripe peaches, bring back to the boil, then cover the pan and simmer for 10–15 minutes until they're almost soft, turning from time to time. Carefully lift out the peaches with a slotted spoon, reserving the liquid. Leave to cool slightly, then remove the skins and put the peaches in a serving dish. Bring the reserved liquid to the boil and bubble for 10 minutes until syrupy. Strain the syrup over the peaches and allow to cool. Cover and chill.

Vanilla Chilled Risotto

900ml (1¹/₂ pints) whole (full-fat) milk

1 vanilla pod, split lengthways

75g (3oz) risotto rice

40g (1¹/₂oz) caster sugar

200ml (7fl oz) double cream

ground cinnamon to sprinkle

Orange Poached Peaches (see Cook's Tip) to serve

1 Put the milk and vanilla pod in a large pan and bring slowly to the boil. Stir in the rice, reduce the heat and simmer gently for about 40 minutes, stirring from time to time, until the rice is soft and most of the liquid has been absorbed. You might need to add a little more milk during the cooking time.

2 Stir in the sugar, remove the vanilla pod and set aside to cool. Once the mixture has cooled, stir in the cream, pour into a large bowl, cover and chill.

3 Just before serving, sprinkle with a little ground cinnamon. Serve with Orange Poached Peaches.

EASY		NUTRITIONAL INFORMATION		Serves
Preparation Time 5 minutes, plus cooling and chilling	**Cooking Time** 40 minutes	**Per Serving** 280 calories, 14g fat (of which 9g saturates), 34g carbohydrate, 0.1g salt	Vegetarian Gluten free	**10**

Sticky Banoffee Pies

150g (5oz) digestive biscuits

75g (3oz) unsalted butter, melted, plus extra to grease

1 tsp ground ginger (optional)

450g (1lb) dulce de leche toffee sauce

4 bananas, peeled, sliced and tossed in the juice of 1 lemon

300ml (½ pint) double cream, lightly whipped

plain chocolate shavings

1 Put the biscuits in a food processor and whiz until they resemble fine crumbs. (Alternatively, put them in a plastic bag and crush with a rolling pin. Transfer to a bowl.) Add the melted butter and ginger, and process, or stir well, for 1 minute to combine.

2 Butter six 10cm (4in) rings or tartlet tins and line with greaseproof paper. Press the biscuit mixture into each ring. Divide the toffee sauce equally among the rings and top with the bananas. Pipe or spoon on the cream, sprinkle with chocolate shavings and chill. Remove from the rings or tins to serve.

Serves 6	EASY		NUTRITIONAL INFORMATION	
	Preparation Time 15 minutes, plus chilling		**Per Serving** 827 calories, 55g fat (of which 32g saturates), 84g carbohydrate, 1.2g salt	Vegetarian

Zabaglione

4 medium egg yolks
100g (3½oz) caster sugar
100ml (3½fl oz) sweet Marsala

1 Heat a pan of water to boiling point. Put the egg yolks and sugar into a heatproof bowl large enough to rest over the pan without touching the base. With the bowl in place, reduce the heat so that the water is just simmering.

2 Using a hand-held electric whisk, whisk the yolks and sugar for 15 minutes until pale, thick and foaming. With the bowl still over the heat, gradually pour in the Marsala, whisking all the time.

3 Pour the zabaglione into four glasses or small coffee cups and serve immediately.

EASY		NUTRITIONAL INFORMATION		Serves
Preparation Time 5 minutes	**Cooking Time** 20 minutes	**Per Serving** 193 calories, 6g fat (of which 2g saturates), 28g carbohydrate, 0g salt	Vegetarian Gluten free • Dairy free	**4**

Cook's Tip

Quark is a smooth soft white cheese, with a texture between yogurt and fromage frais. Fromage frais can be used as an alternative.

Tiramisù

250ml (9fl oz) cold coffee

2 tbsp coffee liqueur, such as Kahlúa or Tia Maria

24 sponge fingers

2 medium eggs, separated

3 tbsp icing sugar

500g (1lb 2oz) quark

1 tsp vanilla extract

cocoa powder to dust

1 Pour the cold coffee and coffee liqueur into a bowl. Dip 12 of the sponge fingers into the liquid, and put into six serving dishes or one large dish.

2 Whisk the egg whites in a clean, grease-free bowl until soft peaks form. In a separate bowl, whisk together the egg yolks, icing sugar, quark and vanilla. Fold in the whites.

3 Spoon half the quark mixture over the sponges. Dip the remaining sponge fingers in the coffee mixture, then put on top. Cover with the remaining quark mixture. Dust with cocoa powder and serve.

Serves 6	EASY		NUTRITIONAL INFORMATION	
	Preparation Time 20 minutes		**Per Serving** 344 calories, 16g fat (of which 4g saturates), 39g carbohydrate, 0.5g salt	Vegetarian

Try Something Different

- -

Use raspberries or other soft berries instead of blueberries.

1 large sponge flan case, 23–25cm (9–10in) diameter

300g (11oz) cream cheese

1 tsp vanilla extract

100g (3½oz) golden caster sugar

150ml (¼ pint) soured cream

2 medium eggs

2 tbsp cornflour

150g (5oz) blueberries

2 tbsp redcurrant jelly

Blueberry Cheesecake

1 Preheat the oven to 180°C (160°C fan oven) mark 4. Use the base of a 20.5cm (8in) springform cake tin to cut out a circle from the flan case, discarding the edges. Grease the tin and line the base with greaseproof paper, then put the flan base into it. Press down with your fingers.

2 Put the cream cheese, vanilla, sugar, soured cream, eggs and cornflour in a food processor, and blend until evenly combined. Pour the mixture over the flan base and shake gently to level. Bake for 45 minutes until just set and pale golden. Turn off the oven and leave the cheesecake inside with the door ajar for about 30 minutes. Cool and chill.

3 To serve, put the blueberries in a pan with the redcurrant jelly and heat through until the jelly has melted and the blueberries have softened slightly – or cook on full power in a 900W microwave for 1 minute. Spoon over the top of the cheesecake. Cool and chill for 15 minutes before serving.

EASY		NUTRITIONAL INFORMATION		Serves
Preparation Time 15 minutes, plus chilling	**Cooking Time** 45 minutes, plus cooling	**Per Serving** 376 calories, 24g fat (of which 14g saturates), 36g carbohydrate, 0.4g salt	Vegetarian	**8**

Toasted Hazelnut Meringue Cake

oil to grease

175g (6oz) skinned hazelnuts, toasted

3 large egg whites

175g (6oz) golden caster sugar

250g (9oz) mascarpone cheese

300ml (½ pint) double cream

3 tbsp whiskey cream liqueur, plus extra to serve

150g (5oz) fresh or frozen raspberries

340g jar redcurrant jelly

1 Preheat the oven to 190°C (170°C fan oven) mark 5. Lightly oil two 18cm (7in) sandwich tins and line the bases with baking parchment. Whiz the hazelnuts in a food processor until finely chopped.

2 Put the egg whites into a clean, grease-free bowl and whisk until stiff peaks form. Whisk in the sugar, a spoonful at a time. Fold in half the nuts using a metal spoon. Divide the mixture between the tins and spread evenly. Bake in the middle of the oven for about 30 minutes, then leave to cool in the tins for 30 minutes.

3 To make the filling, put the mascarpone cheese in a bowl. Beat in the cream and liqueur until smooth. Put the raspberries and redcurrant jelly in a pan and heat gently until the jelly has melted. Sieve, then cool.

4 Use a palette knife to loosen the edges of the meringues, then turn out on to a wire rack. Peel off the baking parchment and discard. Put a large sheet of baking parchment on a board and sit one meringue on top, flat side down. Spread a third of the mascarpone mixture over the meringue, then drizzle with raspberry purée. Top with the other meringue, then cover the whole cake with the rest of the mascarpone mixture and raspberry purée. Sprinkle with the remaining hazelnuts. Carefully put the cake on to a serving plate and drizzle with more liqueur if you like.

Freezing Tips

Freezing the meringue makes it slightly softer but no less tasty.

To freeze Complete the recipe up to the end of step 4 but don't put on serving plate or drizzle with more liqueur. Lift the cake on the baking parchment into the freezer, then freeze until solid. Transfer to a sturdy container and freeze for up to one month.

To use Thaw overnight in the refrigerator, then complete the recipe.

A LITTLE EFFORT		NUTRITIONAL INFORMATION		Serves
Preparation Time 10 minutes	**Cooking Time** about 30 minutes, plus cooling	**Per Serving** 598 calories, 38g fat (of which 16g saturates), 57g carbohydrate, 0.1g salt	Vegetarian Gluten free	**8**

3

Chocolate Treats

Try Something Different

Replace the brandy with Grand Marnier and use orange-flavoured plain chocolate.

Chocolate Crêpes with a Boozy Sauce

100g (3½oz) plain flour, sifted

a pinch of salt

1 medium egg

300ml (½ pint) milk

sunflower oil for frying

50g (2oz) plain chocolate (at least 70% cocoa solids), roughly chopped

100g (3½oz) unsalted butter

100g (3½oz) light muscovado sugar, plus extra to sprinkle

4 tbsp brandy

1 Put the flour and salt in a bowl, make a well in the centre and add the egg. Use a balloon whisk to mix the egg with a little of the flour, then gradually add the milk to make a smooth batter. Cover and leave to stand for about 20 minutes.

2 Pour the batter into a jug. Heat 1 tsp oil in a 23cm (9in) frying pan, then pour in 100ml (3½fl oz) batter, tilting the pan so that the mixture coats the bottom, and fry for 1–2 minutes until golden underneath. Turn carefully and fry the other side. Tip on to a plate, cover with greaseproof paper and repeat with the remaining batter, using more oil as needed.

3 Divide the chocolate among the crêpes. Fold each crêpe in half, then in half again.

4 Put the butter and sugar in a heavy-based frying pan over a low heat. Add the brandy and stir. Slide the crêpes into the pan and cook for 3–4 minutes to melt the chocolate. Serve drizzled with sauce and sprinkled with sugar.

Serves	EASY		NUTRITIONAL INFORMATION	
4	**Preparation Time** 5 minutes, plus standing	**Cooking Time** 10–15 minutes	**Per Serving** 594 calories, 35g fat (of which 17g saturates), 57g carbohydrate, 0.5g salt	Vegetarian

Warm Chocolate Fondants

3 medium eggs, plus 3 egg yolks

50g (2oz) golden caster sugar

175g (6oz) plain chocolate (at least 70% cocoa solids), roughly chopped

150g (5oz) unsalted butter

50g (2oz) plain flour, sifted

6 chocolate truffles

1 Preheat the oven to 200°C (180°C fan oven) mark 6. Put the eggs, egg yolks and sugar in a large bowl and beat with an electric whisk for 8–10 minutes until pale and fluffy. You can do this by hand but it will take a little longer.

2 Meanwhile, melt the chocolate and butter in a heatproof bowl over a pan of gently simmering water, making sure the bowl doesn't touch the water.

3 Gently fold the flour into the egg mixture. Stir a spoonful of egg mixture into the melted chocolate, then gently fold the chocolate mixture into the remaining egg mixture.

4 Put a large spoonful of mixture into each of six 200ml (7fl oz) ramekins. Put a chocolate truffle into the centre of each, taking care not to push it down. Divide the remainder of the mixture among the ramekins to cover the truffle; they should be about three-quarters full. Bake for 10–12 minutes until the top is firm and starting to rise and crack. Serve warm.

EASY		NUTRITIONAL INFORMATION		Serves
Preparation Time about 25 minutes	**Cooking Time** 10–12 minutes	**Per Serving** 502 calories, 37g fat (of which 21g saturates), 39g carbohydrate, 0.5g salt	Vegetarian	**6**

Baked Chocolate and Coffee Custards

300ml (½ pint) milk

150ml (¼ pint) double cream

200g (7oz) plain chocolate (at least 70% cocoa solids), broken into small pieces

4 large egg yolks

1 tbsp caster sugar

3 tbsp very strong coffee

shortbread biscuits to serve

For the topping

125g (4oz) mascarpone cheese

1 tsp icing sugar

grated zest and juice of ½ orange, plus extra zest to decorate

1 Preheat the oven to 170°C (150°C fan oven) mark 3. Put the milk, cream and chocolate in a heavy-based pan, and stir over a gentle heat until melted. Mix the yolks, sugar and coffee together, then pour on the warm chocolate milk. Briefly mix together, then strain through a sieve into a jug. Pour into six 150ml (¼ pint) ovenproof dishes or ramekins.

2 Put the dishes in a large roasting tin, and carefully pour in enough hot tap water to come halfway up the sides of the ramekins. Bake in the oven for 20–25 minutes until the custards are just set and still a little wobbly in the middle – they'll firm up as they cool. Carefully lift out of the roasting tin and leave to cool. Put the dishes on a baking sheet and chill for at least 3 hours.

3 Meanwhile, to make the topping, beat the mascarpone, icing sugar, orange zest and juice together until smooth. Cover and chill for 1–2 hours, or up to 24 hours.

4 To serve, put a spoonful of the mascarpone mixture on top of each custard, and decorate with orange zest. Serve with shortbread biscuits.

EASY		NUTRITIONAL INFORMATION		Serves
Preparation Time 15 minutes, plus minimum 3 hours chilling	**Cooking Time** 30 minutes, plus cooling	**Per Serving** 401 calories, 30g fat (of which 17g saturates), 28g carbohydrate, 0.1g salt	Vegetarian	**6**

Try Something Different

Use flavoured dark chocolate for an unusual twist, such as ginger, mint or even chilli.

Dark Chocolate Soufflés

50g (2oz) plain chocolate (at least 70% cocoa solids), chopped

2 tbsp cornflour

1 tbsp cocoa powder

1 tsp instant coffee granules

4 tbsp golden caster sugar

150ml (¼ pint) skimmed milk

2 medium eggs, separated, plus 1 egg white

1 Preheat the oven to 190°C (170°C fan oven) mark 5, and preheat a baking sheet. Put the chocolate in a pan with the cornflour, cocoa powder, coffee, 1 tbsp caster sugar and the milk. Warm gently to melt the chocolate. Increase the heat and stir until the mixture thickens. Allow to cool a little, then stir in the egg yolks. Cover with damp greaseproof paper.

2 Whisk the egg whites in a clean, grease-free bowl until soft peaks form. Gradually whisk in the remaining caster sugar until the mixture is stiff.

3 Stir one-third of egg whites into the chocolate mixture. Fold in the remaining whites and divide among six 150ml (¼ pint) ramekins. Put the ramekins on the baking sheet and bake for 12 minutes until well risen. Serve immediately.

Serves 6	EASY		NUTRITIONAL INFORMATION	
	Preparation Time 20 minutes	**Cooking Time** about 20 minutes	**Per Serving** 134 calories, 4g fat (of which 2g saturates), 22g carbohydrate, 0.1g salt	Vegetarian Gluten free

Try Something Different

Instead of baguette, use croissants or brioche for a richer pudding.

Chocolate-chunk Bread Pudding

200g (7oz) baguette

100g (3½oz) milk chocolate, roughly chopped, plus 50g (2oz) plain or milk chocolate, in chunks

500g carton fresh custard

150ml (¼ pint) milk

1 large egg, beaten

butter to grease

1 tbsp demerara sugar

50g (2oz) walnuts, finely chopped

single cream to serve (optional)

1 Roughly chop the baguette and put it in a large bowl. Put the chopped milk chocolate in a pan with the custard and milk over a low heat. Stir gently until the chocolate has melted. Beat in the egg.

2 Pour the chocolate mixture over the bread, stir well to coat, then cover and chill for at least 4 hours.

3 Preheat the oven to 180°C (160°C fan oven) mark 4. Spoon the soaked bread into a buttered 1.4 litre (2½ pint), 7.5cm (3in) deep ovenproof dish, then bake for 30–40 minutes.

4 Sprinkle over the demerara sugar, walnuts and chocolate chunks. Return to the oven for 20–30 minutes until lightly set. Serve the pudding warm, with single cream if you like.

EASY		NUTRITIONAL INFORMATION		Serves
Preparation Time	**Cooking Time**	**Per Serving**	Vegetarian	**6**
20 minutes, plus minimum 4 hours chilling	55 minutes–1¼ hours	390 calories, 17g fat (of which 6g saturates), 51g carbohydrate, 0.7g salt		

White Chocolate Mousse Cake

vegetable oil to grease
450g (1lb) white chocolate, roughly chopped
300ml (½ pint) double cream
finely grated zest of 1 large orange
2 tsp orange liqueur, such as Grand Marnier
300g (11oz) full-fat Greek yogurt
halved strawberries, a handful of blueberries and a
handful of unsprayed rose petals to decorate
icing sugar to dust

1 Lightly oil a shallow 20cm (8in) round cake tin and line with baking parchment.

2 Put the chocolate in a large bowl with half the cream. Bring a large pan of water to the boil, remove from the heat and sit the bowl of chocolate and cream on top, making sure the base of the bowl doesn't touch the water. Leave for 20–30 minutes until the chocolate has melted. Don't stir; just leave it to melt.

3 Meanwhile, put the orange zest and liqueur in a small bowl. Set aside to soak. Whip the remaining cream until it just holds its shape.

4 Remove the bowl of melted chocolate from the pan and beat in the yogurt. Fold in the cream with the zest and liqueur mixture. Spoon the mixture into the prepared tin, cover with clingfilm and freeze overnight or for up to one month.

5 One hour before serving, transfer from the freezer to the refrigerator. Unwrap and put on a serving plate. Decorate with fruit and petals and dust lightly with icing sugar.

Serves	A LITTLE EFFORT		NUTRITIONAL INFORMATION	
10	**Preparation Time** 30 minutes, plus overnight freezing	**Cooking Time** 20–30 minutes	**Per Serving** 416 calories, 32g fat (of which 19g saturates), 27g carbohydrate, 0.2g salt	Vegetarian Gluten free

Chocolate and Cherry Amaretti Tart

400g (14oz) pitted bottled or canned morello cherries, drained

3 tbsp brandy, sloe gin or almond-flavoured liqueur

150g (5oz) butter, softened

50g (2oz) icing sugar, plus extra to dust

1 small egg, beaten

225g (8oz) plain flour, plus extra to dust

For the filling

100g (3½oz) plain chocolate, roughly chopped

125g (4oz) butter, softered

125g (4oz) caster sugar

3 large eggs, beaten

125g (4oz) ground almonds

25g (1oz) self-raising flour, sifted

50g (2oz) amaretti biscuits, crushed

75g (3oz) slivered or flaked almonds

1 Put the cherries in a bowl with the brandy, gin or liqueur and leave for 30 minutes. Put the butter, icing sugar and egg in a food processor and whiz until almost smooth. Add the flour and whiz until the mixture begins to form a dough. (Alternatively, rub the fat into the flour by hand or using a pastry cutter, stir in the icing sugar and egg, then the flour.) Knead the pastry lightly, then wrap and chill for 30 minutes.

2 Roll out the pastry on a lightly floured worksurface and line a 23cm (9in) loose-based fluted tart tin. Chill for 20 minutes. Preheat the oven to 200°C (180°C fan oven) mark 6. Line the pastry base with greaseproof paper and baking beans and cook for 15 minutes. Remove the paper and beans and put back in the oven for 5 minutes. Reduce the oven temperature to 150°C (130°C fan oven) mark 2.

3 For the filling, melt the chocolate in a heatproof bowl over a pan of gently simmering water. Stir once or twice until smooth. Cool. In a bowl, beat the butter with the sugar until pale and fluffy. Gradually beat in the eggs, alternating with the almonds and flour. Fold in the melted chocolate and amaretti biscuits. Spoon one-third of the mixture over the base of the pastry case. Spoon the cherries over. Add the remaining filling mixture and spread to cover the cherries. Sprinkle on the almonds and bake for about 1 hour. The tart will have a thin top crust but be soft underneath. Leave in the tin for 10–15 minutes to firm up, then unmould, dust with icing sugar and serve warm.

Freezing Tip

To freeze Complete the recipe but do not dust with icing sugar. Cool completely, wrap and freeze.
To use Thaw at cool room temperature overnight. Warm through at 200°C (180°C fan oven) mark 6 for 10 minutes and dust with icing sugar before serving.

A LITTLE EFFORT		NUTRITIONAL INFORMATION		Serves
Preparation Time 30 minutes, plus 50 minutes chilling	**Cooking Time** 1½ hours, plus 10–15 minutes cooling	**Per Serving** 760 calories, 50g fat (of which 22g saturates), 67g carbohydrate, 0.8g salt	Vegetarian	**8**

Freezing Tip

To freeze Complete the recipe to step 4, wrap, label and freeze.
To use Thaw overnight at cool room temperature. Complete the recipe.

Chocolate and Cherry Gateau

350g (12oz) fresh cherries, pitted, or 400g can pitted cherries, drained, plus extra fresh cherries to serve

3 tbsp dark rum

50g (2oz) almonds, toasted

50g (2oz) plain flour, sifted

350g (12oz) plain chocolate (at least 70% cocoa solids), roughly chopped

3 large eggs, separated

125g (4oz) butter, softened, plus extra to grease

125g (4oz) caster sugar

450ml (³/₄ pint) double cream

chocolate curls (see page 21) and cocoa powder to decorate

single cream to serve (optional)

1 Put the cherries in a bowl with 2 tbsp rum. Cover and soak for at least 6 hours.

2 Whiz the almonds and flour in a food processor until finely ground. Preheat the oven to 180°C (160°C fan oven) mark 4. Grease a 23cm (9in) round deep cake tin and line the base with greaseproof paper.

3 Melt 150g (5oz) chocolate with 3 tbsp water in a bowl over a pan of gently simmering water. Remove from the heat, add the remaining rum and the egg yolks and beat until smooth. Beat the butter and sugar together until pale and fluffy. Stir in the chocolate mixture and fold in the flour and almonds. Whisk the egg whites until soft peaks form, then fold into the chocolate mixture. Pour into the tin and bake for 30–35 minutes until a skewer comes out clean with a few crumbs on it. Cool in the tin for 10 minutes, then turn out on to a wire rack to cool.

4 Put the remaining chocolate in a large bowl. Bring the cream to the boil, pour over the chocolate, leave for 5 minutes, then stir until melted. Allow to cool, then, using an electric whisk, beat the mixture until thick and pale. Clean the cake tin and return the cake to the tin. Spoon the soaked cherries and any juice over the cake. Spread the chocolate cream on top, smooth the surface, cover and chill for at least 2 hours.

5 Decorate with chocolate curls, dust with cocoa and serve with fresh cherries and cream if you like.

Serves 12	EASY		NUTRITIONAL INFORMATION	
	Preparation Time 1 hour, plus 8 hours soaking and chilling	**Cooking Time** 45 minutes, plus cooling	**Per Serving** 537 calories, 41g fat (of which 23g saturates), 38g carbohydrate, 0.2g salt	Vegetarian

Decadent Chocolate Cake

225g (8oz) unsalted butter, softened, plus extra to grease
300g (11oz) plain chocolate, broken into pieces
225g (8oz) golden caster sugar
225g (8oz) ground almonds
8 large eggs, separated
125g (4oz) fresh brown breadcrumbs
4 tbsp apricot jam (optional)

For the ganache

175g (6oz) plain chocolate, broken into pieces
75g (3oz) butter, softened
4 tbsp double cream

1 Preheat the oven to 180°C (160°C fan oven) mark 4. Grease a 23cm (9in) springform cake tin and line the base with greaseproof paper. Melt the chocolate in a heatproof bowl over a pan of gently simmering water. Remove from the heat. Put the butter and sugar in a large bowl and beat until pale and creamy. Add the almonds, egg yolks and breadcrumbs and beat well. Slowly add the chocolate and carefully stir it in, taking care not to overmix as the chocolate may seize up. Put the egg whites in a clean, grease-free bowl and whisk until stiff peaks form. Add half the whites to the chocolate mixture and fold in lightly using a large metal spoon. Carefully fold in the remainder. Pour into the tin and level the surface. Bake for 1 hour 20 minutes or until the cake is firm to the touch and a skewer inserted into the centre comes out clean. Leave in the tin for 5 minutes, then transfer to a rack for 2–3 hours to cool completely.

2 Put the jam, if using, in a pan and melt over a low heat. Brush the jam over the cooled cake.

3 To make the ganache, melt the chocolate, butter and cream in a heatproof bowl over a pan of gently simmering water. Stir just once, until smooth. Either raise the cake off the worksurface on the upturned tin or put it (still on the rack) on to a tray to catch the drips. Pour the ganache over the centre and tip the cake to let it run down the sides evenly, or spread it with a palette knife. Slice and serve with cream if you like.

A LITTLE EFFORT		NUTRITIONAL INFORMATION		Serves
Preparation Time 30 minutes	**Cooking Time** 1½ hours, plus 2–3 hours cooling	**Per Serving** 693 calories, 49g fat (of which 23g saturates), 54g carbohydrate, 0.7g salt	Vegetarian	**12**

Chocolate and Hazelnut Meringues

125g (4oz) hazelnuts

125g (4oz) caster sugar

75g (3oz) plain chocolate (at least 70% cocoa solids)

2 medium egg whites

300ml (1/2 pint) double cream

redcurrants, blackberries and chocolate shavings to decorate

physalis (Cape gooseberries) dipped in caramel (see Cook's Tips) to serve (optional)

1 To make the meringues, preheat the oven to 110°C (90°C fan oven) mark 1/4. Line two baking sheets with non-stick baking parchment. Spread the hazelnuts over a baking sheet. Toast under a hot grill until golden brown, turning them frequently. Put the hazelnuts in a clean teatowel and rub off the skins. Put the nuts in a food processor with 3 tbsp of the sugar and process to a fine powder. Add the chocolate and pulse until roughly chopped.

2 In a large grease-free bowl, whisk the egg whites until stiff; whisk in the remaining caster sugar a spoonful at a time until the mixture is stiff and shiny. Fold in the nut mixture.

3 Spoon the mixture on to the prepared baking sheets, making small rough mounds about 9cm (3 1/2in) in diameter. Bake for about 45 minutes until the meringues will just peel off the paper. Gently push in the base of each meringue to form a deep hollow; put back in the oven for 1 1/4 hours or until crisp and dry. Leave to cool.

4 Whip the cream until it just holds its shape; spoon three-quarters on to the meringues. Leave in the refrigerator to soften for up to 2 hours.

5 Decorate the meringues with the remaining cream, fruit and chocolate shavings. Serve immediately, with caramel-dipped physalis if you like.

Serves	A LITTLE EFFORT		NUTRITIONAL INFORMATION	
6	**Preparation Time** 25 minutes, plus 2 hours softening	**Cooking Time** 2 hours, plus cooling	**Per Serving** 520 calories, 42g fat (of which 19g saturates), 32g carbohydrate, 0.1g salt	Vegetarian Gluten free

Cook's Tip

White Chocolate Custard: put 4 tbsp custard powder and 4 tsp sugar in a bowl; add enough of 450ml (³/₄ pint) skimmed milk to make a smooth paste. Heat the remaining milk until almost boiling, pour into the custard powder, then put back in the pan. Add 40g (1¹/₂oz) white chocolate drops and stir until the chocolate has melted and the custard thickened.

Chocolate Puddings with White Chocolate Custard

125g (4oz) half-fat butter, plus extra to grease

75g (3oz) light muscovado sugar

75g (3oz) self-raising flour

¹/₂ tsp baking powder

2 tbsp cocoa powder, plus extra to dust

25g (1oz) hazelnuts, lightly toasted, skinned and roughly chopped (see pages 22–23)

25g (1oz) plain chocolate (at least 70% cocoa solids), roughly chopped

2 large eggs, beaten

White Chocolate Custard (see Cook's Tip) to serve

1 Preheat the oven to 180°C (160°C fan oven) mark 4. Grease six 150ml (¹/₄ pint) ramekins and line the bases with non-stick baking parchment.

2 Put the butter and sugar in a pan and heat gently until combined. Cool.

3 Sift the flour, baking powder and cocoa powder into a bowl. Stir in the nuts and chocolate. Make a well in the centre; pour in the butter mixture and eggs, and beat well. Pour the mixture into the prepared ramekins and bake for 20–25 minutes until just firm to the touch. Cool slightly and turn out; keep warm.

4 Trim the top from each pudding and place upside down on six serving plates. Dust with cocoa powder, pour the White Chocolate Custard around and serve immediately.

EASY		NUTRITIONAL INFORMATION		Serves
Preparation Time 20 minutes	**Cooking Time** 20–25 minutes	**Per Serving** 347 calories, 20g fat (of which 10g saturates), 37g carbohydrate, 0.6g salt	Vegetarian	**6**

Get Ahead

Complete the recipe to the end of step 4 up to one day ahead. Cover and chill until needed.
To use Complete the recipe.

White Chocolate Mousse

100ml (3½fl oz) full-fat milk

1 cinnamon stick

250g (9oz) white chocolate, broken into pieces

300ml (½ pint) double cream

3 large egg whites

50g (2oz) plain chocolate

a little cocoa powder and ground cinnamon to decorate

1 Put the milk and cinnamon stick in a small pan and warm over a medium heat until the milk is almost boiling. Take the pan off the heat and set aside.

2 Melt the white chocolate in a heatproof bowl over a pan of gently simmering water. Take the bowl off the pan and leave to cool a little.

3 Strain the warm milk on to the melted chocolate and stir together until completely smooth. Leave to cool for 10 minutes.

4 Whip the cream until it just begins to hold its shape. Whisk the egg whites until soft peaks form. Fold the whipped cream into the chocolate mixture with a large metal spoon, then carefully fold in the egg whites. Spoon the mixture into six 150ml (¼ pint) bowls or glasses and chill for 4 hours or overnight.

5 Pull a vegetable peeler across the edge of the plain chocolate to make curls. Sprinkle over the mousse. Dust with cocoa powder and a pinch of cinnamon.

Serves 6	EASY		NUTRITIONAL INFORMATION	
	Preparation Time 15 minutes, plus minimum 4 hours chilling	**Cooking Time** 15 minutes	**Per Serving** 515 calories, 41g fat (of which 25g saturates), 31g carbohydrate, 0.2g salt	Vegetarian Gluten free

Try Something Different

Turn this into a fun chocolate fondue by offering different fruits for dunking, such as mango and pineapple chunks, raspberries or even marshmallows – provide a pile of cocktail sticks for easy dunking.

Chocolate-dipped Strawberries

100g (3½oz) milk chocolate, broken into chunks
100g (3½oz) white chocolate, broken into chunks
100g (3½oz) plain chocolate (at least 70% cocoa solids), broken into chunks
700g (1½lb) strawberries

1 Put each type of chocolate side by side in a single heatproof bowl, keeping each type as separate as you can.

2 Melt the chocolate over a pan of gently simmering water, then dip each strawberry into the chocolate, holding it by its stalk. Arrange the strawberries in a shallow bowl to serve. Alternatively let everyone dunk the berries themselves.

EASY		NUTRITIONAL INFORMATION		Serves
Preparation Time 10 minutes	**Cooking Time** about 10 minutes	**Per Serving** 291 calories, 15g fat (of which 9g saturates), 37g carbohydrate, 0.1g salt	Vegetarian Gluten free	**6**

Warming Puddings

Cook's Tip

Panettone is a yeasted fruit cake that is a traditional
Christmas treat in Italy and is most widely available around
Christmas time. If you can't find it, use brioche or
cinnamon and raisin bread.

Panettone Pudding

50g (2oz) butter, at room temperature,
plus extra to grease

500g (1lb 2oz) panettone (see Cook's Tip), cut into slices
about 5mm (¼ in) thick

3 large eggs, beaten

150g (5oz) golden caster sugar

300ml (½ pint) full-fat milk

150ml (¼ pint) double cream

grated zest of 1 orange

1 Butter a 2 litre (3½ pint) ovenproof dish. Lightly
butter the panettone slices, then tear them into
pieces and arrange in the dish.

2 Mix the eggs with the sugar in a large bowl, then
whisk in the milk, cream and orange zest. Pour the
mixture over the buttered panettone and leave to
soak for 20 minutes. Preheat the oven to 170°C
(150°C fan oven) mark 3.

3 Put the dish in a roasting tin and pour in enough
hot water to come halfway up the sides. Bake for
35–45 minutes until the pudding is just set in the
middle and golden.

EASY		NUTRITIONAL INFORMATION		Serves
Preparation Time 20 minutes, plus 20 minutes soaking	**Cooking Time** 35–45 minutes	**Per Serving** 581 calories, 29g fat (of which 16g saturates), 73g carbohydrate, 0.9g salt	Vegetarian	**6**

Bread and Butter Pudding

50g (2oz) butter, softened, plus extra to grease

275g (10oz) white farmhouse bread, cut into 1cm (½in) slices, crusts removed

50g (2oz) raisins or sultanas

3 medium eggs

450ml (¾ pint) milk

3 tbsp golden icing sugar, plus extra to dust

1 Lightly butter four 300ml (½ pint) gratin dishes or one 1.1 litre (2 pint) ovenproof dish. Butter the bread, then cut into quarters to make triangles. Arrange the bread in the dish(es) and sprinkle with the raisins.

2 Beat the eggs, milk and sugar in a bowl. Pour the mixture over the bread and leave to soak for 10 minutes. Preheat the oven to 180°C (160°C fan oven) mark 4.

3 Put the pudding(s) in the oven and bake for 30–40 minutes. Dust with icing sugar to serve.

Serves	EASY		NUTRITIONAL INFORMATION	
4	**Preparation Time** 10 minutes, plus 10 minutes soaking	**Cooking Time** 30-40 minutes	**Per Serving** 450 calories, 13g fat (of which 5g saturates), 70g carbohydrate, 1.1g salt	Vegetarian

340g pack sweet pastry

75g (3oz) self-raising flour, sifted

finely grated zest of $\frac{1}{2}$ lemon

50g (2oz) unsalted butter, chilled and cut into cubes

50g (2oz) light muscovado sugar

25g (1oz) ground almonds

350g jar mincemeat

brandy butter or thick cream to serve

Mincemeat Streusel

1 Preheat the oven to 180°C (160°C fan oven) mark 4. Grease a 33 x 10cm (13 x 4in) fluted rectangular tin and line the base with greaseproof paper.

2 Roll out the pastry and use to line the tin. Prick the pastry with a fork, cover with baking parchment and baking beans and bake for 15 minutes. Remove the parchment and beans and bake for a further 15 minutes, then leave to cool for 5 minutes. Do not turn off the oven.

3 Meanwhile, to make the streusel topping, put the flour and lemon zest in a bowl. Rub in the butter until the mixture resembles crumbs. Stir in the sugar and ground almonds.

4 Spread the mincemeat evenly over the pastry, and sprinkle the streusel on top. Bake for 15 minutes until the topping is golden. Leave to cool for 30 minutes, then remove from the tin. Slice and serve warm with brandy butter or cream.

EASY		NUTRITIONAL INFORMATION		Serves
Preparation Time 15 minutes	**Cooking Time** 45 minutes, plus cooling	**Per Serving** 429 calories, 21g fat (of which 3g saturates), 61g carbohydrate, 0.3g salt	Vegetarian	**8**

Try Something Different

Use apples instead of pears.

Pear and Blackberry Crumble

450g (1lb) pears, peeled, cored and chopped, tossed with the juice of 1 lemon

225g (8oz) golden caster sugar

1 tsp mixed spice

450g (1lb) blackberries

100g (3½oz) butter, chopped, plus extra to grease

225g (8oz) plain flour

75g (3oz) ground almonds

cream, custard or ice cream to serve

1 Put the pears and lemon juice in a bowl, add 100g (3½oz) of the sugar and the mixed spice, then add the blackberries and toss thoroughly to coat.

2 Preheat the oven to 200°C (180°C fan oven) mark 6. Lightly butter a 1.8 litre (3¼ pint) shallow dish, then carefully tip the fruit into the dish in an even layer.

3 Put the butter, flour, ground almonds and the remaining sugar in a food processor and pulse until the mixture begins to resemble breadcrumbs. Tip into a bowl and bring parts of it together with your hands to make lumps. Spoon the crumble topping evenly over the fruit, then bake for 35–45 minutes until the fruit is tender and the crumble is golden and bubbling. Serve with cream, custard or ice cream.

Serves 6	EASY		NUTRITIONAL INFORMATION	
	Preparation Time 20 minutes	**Cooking Time** 35–45 minutes	**Per Serving** 525 calories, 21g fat (of which 9g saturates), 81g carbohydrate, 0.3g salt	Vegetarian

Try Something Different

- -

Replace the jam with ginger conserve and use ginger ice cream instead of vanilla.

1 large sponge flan case, 25.5cm (10in) diameter

5 tbsp orange juice

7 tbsp jam – any kind

1.5 litre tub vanilla ice cream

6 large egg whites

a pinch of cream of tartar

a pinch of salt

275g (10oz) golden caster sugar

Baked Alaska

1. Put the flan case on an ovenproof plate. Spoon the orange juice over the sponge, then spread over the jam. Scoop the ice cream on top of the jam, then put in the freezer for at least 30 minutes.

2. Put the egg whites into a large, clean, grease-free bowl and whisk until stiff. Beat in the cream of tartar and salt. Use a large spoon to fold in the sugar, 1 tbsp at a time, then whisk until very thick and shiny.

3. Spoon the meringue over the ice cream to cover, making sure that the meringue is sealed to the flan case edge all the way round. Freeze for at least 1 hour or overnight.

4. Preheat the oven to 230°C (210°C fan oven) mark 8. Bake for 3–4 minutes until the meringue is tinged golden brown. Serve immediately. If the Baked Alaska has been in the freezer overnight, bake and leave to stand for about 15 minutes before serving.

Serves 8	EASY		NUTRITIONAL INFORMATION	
	Preparation Time 30 minutes, plus minimum 1½ hours freezing	**Cooking Time** 3–4 minutes	**Per Serving** 659 calories, 30g fat (of which 17g saturates), 91g carbohydrate, 0.5g salt	Vegetarian

Try Something Different

For an autumnal clafoutis, replace the cherries with blackberries, the kirsch with blackberry or blackcurrant liqueur and the vanilla with ¼ tsp ground cinnamon.

Cherry Clafoutis

350g (12oz) cherries, pitted

3 tbsp Kirsch

125g (4oz) golden caster sugar

4 large eggs

25g (1oz) plain flour, sifted

150ml (¼ pint) milk

150ml (¼ pint) double cream

1 tsp vanilla extract

a little butter to grease

1 Put the cherries in a bowl with the Kirsch and 1 tbsp sugar. Mix together, cover and set aside for 1 hour.

2 Meanwhile, whisk together the eggs, 100g (3½oz) of the sugar and the flour in a bowl. Put the milk and cream into a small pan and bring to the boil. Pour on to the egg mixture and whisk until combined. Stir in the vanilla extract, then strain into a bowl. Cover and set aside for 30 minutes. Preheat the oven to 180°C (160°C fan oven) mark 4.

3 Lightly butter a 1.7 litre (3 pint) shallow ovenproof dish, and sprinkle with the remaining caster sugar. Spoon the Kirsch-soaked cherries into the dish. Whisk the batter again, then pour it over the cherries. Bake for 50 minutes–1 hour until golden and just set. Serve warm.

EASY		NUTRITIONAL INFORMATION		Serves
Preparation Time 20 minutes, plus 1 hour soaking	**Cooking Time** about 1 hour	**Per Serving** 326 calories, 18g fat (of which 10g saturates), 33g carbohydrate, 0.2g salt	Vegetarian	**6**

Hot Pear and White Chocolate Puddings

100g (3½oz) butter, softened, plus extra to grease
100g (3½oz) self-raising flour, sifted
100g (3½oz) light muscovado sugar
1 tsp cocoa powder
1 medium egg
2–3 drops of almond extract
50g (2oz) white chocolate, chopped
2 ripe pears
25g (1oz) flaked almonds

1 Preheat the oven to 180°C (160°C fan oven) mark 4. Lightly grease four 250ml (9fl oz) ramekins.

2 Put half the butter, half the flour and half the muscovado sugar in a bowl. Add the cocoa powder, egg and almond extract, and beat together until smooth. Divide the mixture among the prepared ramekins. Scatter half the chocolate on top.

3 Peel, core and chop the pears, and divide among the ramekins.

4 In a bowl, rub together the remaining butter, flour and sugar until the mixture resembles breadcrumbs. Stir in the flaked almonds and the remaining chocolate, then sprinkle over the pears and bake for 20 minutes or until golden. Serve hot.

Serves 4	EASY		NUTRITIONAL INFORMATION	
	Preparation Time 20 minutes	**Cooking Time** 20 minutes	**Per Serving** 524 calories, 30g fat (of which 16g saturates), 61g carbohydrate, 0.5g salt	Vegetarian

Sticky Toffee Puddings

1 tbsp golden syrup

1 tbsp black treacle

150g (5oz) butter, softened

25g (1oz) pecan nuts or walnuts, finely ground

75g (3oz) self-raising flour

125g (4oz) caster sugar

2 large eggs, beaten

cream or custard to serve

1 Preheat the oven to 180°C (160°C fan oven) mark 4. Put the syrup, treacle and 25g (1oz) butter in a bowl and beat until smooth. Divide the mixture among four 150ml (¼ pint) timbales or ramekins and set aside.

2 Put the nuts in a bowl, sift in the flour and mix together well.

3 Put the remaining butter and the sugar in a food processor and blend briefly. (Alternatively, use an electric hand mixer.) Add the eggs and the flour mixture and blend or mix again for 30 seconds. Spoon the mixture into the timbales or ramekins, covering the syrup mixture on the bottom. Bake for 25–30 minutes until risen and golden.

4 Remove the puddings from the oven and leave to rest for 5 minutes, then unmould on to warmed serving plates. Serve immediately with cream or custard.

EASY		NUTRITIONAL INFORMATION		Serves
Preparation Time 20 minutes	**Cooking Time** 25–30 minutes, plus 5 minutes resting	**Per Serving** 565 calories, 38g fat (of which 21g saturates), 53g carbohydrate, 0.9g salt	Vegetarian	**4**

Rice Pudding

butter to grease

125g (4oz) short-grain pudding rice

1.1 litres (2 pints) whole (full-fat) milk

50g (2oz) golden caster sugar

1 tsp vanilla extract

grated zest of 1 orange (optional)

freshly grated nutmeg to taste

1 Preheat the oven to 170°C (150°C fan oven) mark 3. Lightly butter a 1.7 litre (3 pint) ovenproof dish. Add the rice, milk, sugar, vanilla extract and orange zest, if using, and stir everything together. Grate the nutmeg over the top of the mixture.

2 Bake the pudding in the middle of the oven for 1½ hours or until the top is golden brown.

Serves 6	EASY		NUTRITIONAL INFORMATION	
	Preparation Time 5 minutes	**Cooking Time** 1½ hours	**Per Serving** 239 calories, 8g fat (of which 5g saturates), 34g carbohydrate, 0.2g salt	Vegetarian Gluten free

Rustic Blackberry and Apple Pie

200g (7oz) plain flour, plus extra to dust

125g (4oz) chilled unsalted butter, diced

1 medium egg, beaten

75g (3oz) golden caster sugar, plus 3 tbsp

pinch of salt

500g (1lb 2oz) eating apples, quartered, cored and cut into chunky wedges

300g (11oz) blackberries

¼ tsp ground cinnamon

juice of 1 small lemon

1 Pulse the flour and butter in a food processor until it resembles coarse crumbs. (Alternatively, rub the butter into the flour by hand or using a pastry cutter.) Add the egg, 2 tbsp sugar and the salt, and pulse again to combine, or stir in. Wrap in clingfilm and chill for at least 15 minutes. Meanwhile, preheat the oven to 200°C (180°C fan oven) mark 6.

2 Put the apples, blackberries, 75g (3oz) sugar, the cinnamon and lemon juice in a bowl and toss together, making sure the sugar dissolves in the juice.

3 Grease a 25.5cm (10in) enamel or metal pie dish. Using a lightly floured rolling pin, roll out the pastry on a large sheet of baking parchment to a 30.5cm (12in) circle. Lift up the paper, upturn the pastry on to the pie dish and peel away the paper.

4 Put the prepared fruit in the centre of the pie dish and fold the pastry edges up and over the fruit. Sprinkle with the remaining sugar and bake for 40 minutes or until the fruit is tender and the pastry golden.

EASY		NUTRITIONAL INFORMATION		Serves
Preparation Time 25 minutes, plus minimum 15 minutes chilling	**Cooking Time** 40 minutes	**Per Serving** 372 calories, 19g fat (of which 11g saturates), 49g carbohydrate, 0.4g salt	Vegetarian	**6**

Try Something Different

Replace the lemon with orange, the pecans with walnut halves and the whiskey with Cointreau.

Maple Pecan Pie

250g (9oz) plain flour, sifted

a large pinch of salt

225g (8oz) unsalted butter, cubed and chilled

100g (3½oz) light muscovado sugar

125g (4oz) dates, stoned and roughly chopped

grated zest and juice of ½ lemon

100ml (3½fl oz) maple syrup, plus 6 tbsp extra

1 tsp vanilla extract

4 medium eggs

300g (11oz) pecan nut halves

300ml (½ pint) double cream

2 tbsp bourbon whiskey

1 Put the flour and salt in a food processor. Add 125g (4oz) of the butter and whiz to fine crumbs; add 2 tbsp water and whiz until the mixture just comes together. Wrap in clingfilm and chill for 30 minutes. Use to line a 28 x 4cm (11 x 1½ in) loose-bottomed tart tin, then cover and chill for 30 minutes. Preheat the oven to 200°C (180°C fan oven) mark 6.

2 Prick the pastry all over, cover with greaseproof paper and fill with baking beans. Bake for 25 minutes, then remove the paper and beans and bake for a further 5 minutes or until the base is dry and light golden.

3 Meanwhile, whiz the rest of the butter in a food processor to soften. Add the sugar and dates, and whiz to cream together. Add the lemon zest and juice, 100ml (3½fl oz) maple syrup, vanilla extract, eggs and 200g (7oz) nuts. Whiz until the nuts are finely chopped – the mixture will look curdled. Pour into the pastry case and top with the rest of the nuts.

4 Bake for 40–45 minutes until almost set in the middle. Cover with greaseproof paper for the last 10 minutes if the nuts turn very dark. Cool slightly before removing from the tin, then brush with 4 tbsp maple syrup. Lightly whip the cream with the whiskey and 2 tbsp maple syrup; serve with the pie.

Serves	EASY		NUTRITIONAL INFORMATION	
10	**Preparation Time** 40 minutes, plus 1 hour chilling	**Cooking Time** 1¼ hours	**Per Serving** 748 calories, 57g fat (of which 24g saturates), 51g carbohydrate, 0.6g salt	Vegetarian

Try Something Different

- -

Steamed Jam Sponge Puddings: put 4 tbsp raspberry or blackberry jam into the bottom of the basins instead of the syrup.

Steamed Chocolate Sponge Puddings: omit the golden syrup. Blend 4 tbsp cocoa powder with 2 tbsp hot water, then gradually beat into the creamed mixture before adding the eggs.

Steamed Syrup Sponge Puddings

125g (4oz) butter, softened, plus extra to grease

3 tbsp golden syrup

125g (4oz) golden caster sugar

few drops of vanilla extract

2 medium eggs, beaten

175g (6oz) self-raising flour, sifted

about 3 tbsp milk

custard or cream to serve

1 Half-fill a steamer or large pan with water and put it on to boil. Grease four 300ml (½ pint) basins or a 900ml (1½ pint) pudding basin and spoon the golden syrup into the bottom.

2 In a bowl, cream the butter and sugar together until pale and fluffy. Stir in the vanilla extract. Add the eggs, a little at a time, beating well after each addition.

3 Using a metal spoon, fold in half the flour, then fold in the rest with enough milk to give a dropping consistency. Spoon the mixture into the prepared pudding basin(s).

4 Cover with greased and pleated greaseproof paper and foil, and secure with string. Steam for 35 minutes for individual puddings or 1½ hours for one large pudding, checking the water level from time to time and topping up with boiling water as necessary. Turn out on to warmed plates and serve with custard or cream.

EASY		NUTRITIONAL INFORMATION		Serves
Preparation Time 20 minutes	**Cooking Time** 35 minutes or 1½ hours	**Per Serving** 580 calories, 29g fat (of which 17g saturates), 76g carbohydrate, 0.7g salt	Vegetarian	**4**

Try Something Different

- -

Use apricots instead of plums, and white wine instead of red.

150g (5oz) demerara sugar

a pinch of salt

175g (6oz) polenta

25g (1oz) butter

700g (1½ lb) plums, stoned and quartered

1 tsp ground cinnamon

150ml (¼ pint) red wine

150g (5oz) crème fraîche

Polenta and Plum Gratin

1 Line a baking sheet with greaseproof paper. Bring 900ml (1½ pints) water to the boil, and add 25g (1oz) of the sugar and a pinch of salt. Gradually add the polenta, stirring constantly for 2–4 minutes.

2 Stir in the butter, then spread the polenta in a layer about 1cm (½in) thick on the baking sheet. Cover with greaseproof paper and cool.

3 Melt 50g (2oz) of the sugar in a pan over a medium heat until golden, then add the plums, cinnamon, wine and 50ml (2fl oz) water. Simmer for 2–3 minutes until the caramel has dissolved and the plums are tender.

4 Preheat the grill. Cut the polenta into large triangles and put in a deep 1.7 litre (3 pint) heatproof dish. Pour the warm plums over. Dot with the crème fraîche and sprinkle the remaining sugar over the top. Grill for 7 minutes or until golden, then serve.

Serves	EASY		NUTRITIONAL INFORMATION	
6	**Preparation Time** 10 minutes, plus cooling	**Cooking Time** about 20 minutes	**Per Serving** 390 calories, 15g fat (of which 9g saturates), 58g carbohydrate, 0.1g salt	Vegetarian Gluten free

Try Something Different

Replace 1 lemon with a large lime for an added citrus twist.

Saucy Hot Lemon Puddings

50g (2oz) butter, plus extra to grease
125g (4oz) golden caster sugar
finely grated zest and juice of 2 lemons
2 medium eggs, separated
50g (2oz) self-raising flour, sifted
300ml (½ pint) semi-skimmed milk

1 Preheat the oven to 190°C (170°C fan oven) mark 5. Lightly grease four 200ml (7fl oz) ovenproof cups or glasses.

2 In a bowl, cream the butter, sugar and lemon zest together until pale and fluffy. Beat in the egg yolks, then the flour, until combined. Stir in the milk and lemon juice – the mixture will curdle, but don't panic.

3 In a clean, grease-free bowl, whisk the egg whites until soft peaks form, then fold into the lemon mixture. (The mixture will still look curdled – don't worry.) Divide among the four cups and stand them in a roasting tin.

4 Add enough boiling water to the tin to come halfway up the sides of the cups, and bake the puddings for 35–40 minutes until spongy and light golden. If you like softer tops, cover the entire tin with foil. When cooked, the puddings will have separated into a tangy lemon custard layer on the bottom, with a light sponge on top. Serve immediately.

EASY		NUTRITIONAL INFORMATION		Serves
Preparation Time 15–20 minutes	**Cooking Time** 35–40 minutes	**Per Serving** 323 calories, 16g fat (of which 9g saturates), 40g carbohydrate, 0.4g salt	Vegetarian	**4**

American-style Plum Cobbler

900g (2lb) plums, halved and stoned
150g (5oz) golden caster sugar, plus 3 tbsp
1 tbsp cornflour
250g (9oz) self-raising flour
100g (3½oz) chilled unsalted butter, diced
175ml (6fl oz) buttermilk or whole natural yogurt

1 Preheat the oven to 200°C (180°C fan oven) mark 6. Cut the plums into chunky wedges. Tip into an ovenproof dish measuring 25.5 x 18 x 7.5cm (10 x 7 x 3in) and toss together with 3 tbsp sugar and the cornflour.

2 Whiz the flour, butter and 100g (3½oz) sugar in a food processor until the mixture forms fine crumbs. (Alternatively, rub the fat into the flour by hand or using a pastry cutter, then stir in the sugar.) Add the buttermilk or yogurt and blend for a few seconds until just combined.

3 Scatter clumps of the dough over the plums, leaving some of the fruit exposed. Sprinkle the cobbler with the remaining sugar and bake for 40 minutes or until the fruit is tender and the topping is pale golden.

Try Something Different

Toss the plums with the grated zest of ½ orange before baking, and add the grated zest of the remaining ½ orange to the cobbler mixture along with the buttermilk.

EASY		NUTRITIONAL INFORMATION		Serves
Preparation Time 25 minutes	**Cooking Time** 40 minutes	**Per Serving** 451 calories, 15g fat (of which 9g saturates), 76g carbohydrate, 0.3g salt	Vegetarian	**6**

5

Ices and Iced Desserts

Try Something Different

- -

Use canned apricots and canned raspberries instead of peaches and cherries.

Peach and Black Cherry Granita

400g can peach slices in syrup
100g (3½oz) golden caster sugar
4 tbsp lemon juice
400g can pitted black cherries in syrup

1 Drain the peaches and keep the syrup in a measuring jug. Add cold water to the fruit syrup to make it up to 300ml (½ pint).

2 Whiz the peaches in a food processor or blender until smooth. Add half the sugar and half the lemon juice; whiz for a few more seconds. Add the reserved syrup and whiz again to combine.

3 Pour the mixture into a shallow freezerproof container and cover with a tight-fitting lid, then freeze for 2 hours.

4 Repeat steps 1 to 3 with the cherries and the remaining sugar and lemon juice.

5 The mixtures should have started to freeze around the sides and base after 2 hours, so take a large fork and mash the unfrozen mixture into the frozen. Cover and put back in the freezer for a further 1 hour, then mash once more.

6 Spoon alternate layers of peach and cherry granita into six sundae glasses and serve immediately. Alternatively, cover and store the granitas in the freezer for up to three months. To serve, put the granitas in the refrigerator for 30 minutes before serving to soften slightly.

Serves 6	EASY		NUTRITIONAL INFORMATION	
	Preparation Time 15 minutes, plus 3 hours freezing		**Per Serving** 150 calories, trace fat, 39g carbohydrate, 0g salt	Vegetarian Dairy free • Gluten free

Cook's Tip

If you make the ice cream in the morning and eat it later on that day, it will have the perfect 'soft scoop' texture. If it's been in the freezer for longer, you'll need to take it out 20 minutes before slicing to allow it to soften.

Easy Vanilla Ice Cream

300ml (½ pint) double cream

218g can condensed milk

200g carton fresh custard

2 tbsp vanilla extract

crisp sweet biscuits or wafers to serve

1 Line a 900g (2lb) loaf tin or plastic box with clingfilm. Pour the cream into a bowl and whisk until soft peaks form. Stir in the condensed milk, custard and vanilla extract. Pour the mixture into the lined tin and freeze for 6 hours.

2 To serve, invert the ice cream on to a plate and remove the clingfilm. Slice and serve with biscuits or wafers.

EASY	NUTRITIONAL INFORMATION		Serves
Preparation Time 15 minutes, plus 6 hours freezing	**Per Serving** 389 calories, 30g fat (of which 18g saturates), 26g carbohydrate, 0.2g salt	Vegetarian Gluten free	**6**

Cook's Tip

If you're using an ice-cream maker, add the whisked egg white halfway through churning, which will give the sorbet a creamier texture.

Orange Sorbet

grated zest of 3 oranges and juice of 6 oranges – you'll need around 600ml (1 pint)

200g (7oz) golden granulated sugar

1 tbsp orange flower water

1 medium egg white

Medjool dates, sliced, and 1 orange, cut into segments, to decorate

1 Pour 300ml (½ pint) water into a large pan, add the orange zest and sugar, and bring slowly to the boil. Stir occasionally with a wooden spoon to dissolve the sugar. Simmer for 5 minutes. Leave to cool for 1–2 minutes, then strain the syrup into a clean bowl.

2 Strain the orange juice into the cooled syrup and stir in the orange flower water. Chill for 30 minutes.

3 Pour the mixture into a shallow 18cm (7in) square freezerproof container and freeze for 3 hours until slushy. Whisk the egg white until stiff, then fold into the mixture. Put the sorbet back in the freezer and freeze until solid – about 2 hours or overnight.

4 Put the sorbet in the refrigerator for 15–20 minutes before serving to soften slightly. Decorate with Medjool dates and orange segments.

EASY		NUTRITIONAL INFORMATION		Serves
Preparation Time 20 minutes, plus chilling and 5 hours freezing	**Cooking Time** 10 minutes	**Per Serving** 169 calories, trace fat, 44g carbohydrate, 0.1g salt	Vegetarian Dairy free • Gluten free	**6**

Cook's Tip

Lemon Filling: mix 2 tbsp cornflour with 1 tbsp water, then stir in 4 large egg yolks, 100g (3½oz) golden caster sugar, the grated zest and juice of 1 lemon and 1 lime. Bring 125ml (4fl oz) milk to the boil, stir in the cornflour and stir over a low heat until thick. Tip into a bowl, cover with wet greaseproof paper and cool. Whip 300ml (½ pint) double cream until soft peaks form, then gently fold into the filling.

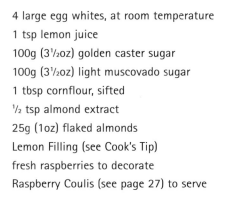

4 large egg whites, at room temperature

1 tsp lemon juice

100g (3½oz) golden caster sugar

100g (3½oz) light muscovado sugar

1 tbsp cornflour, sifted

½ tsp almond extract

25g (1oz) flaked almonds

Lemon Filling (see Cook's Tip)

fresh raspberries to decorate

Raspberry Coulis (see page 27) to serve

Iced Lemon Meringue

1 Preheat the oven to 140°C (120°C fan oven) mark 1. Cut out three 35.5 x 20.5cm (14 x 8in) rectangles of baking parchment and put on a baking sheet. Whisk the egg whites until soft peaks form. Add the lemon juice and whisk until stiff. Whisk in the sugars, 1 tbsp at a time, until glossy. Beat in 1 tbsp boiling water, then fold in the cornflour and almond extract. Divide among the rectangles, leaving a 10cm (4in) border. Reserve 1 tbsp almonds; sprinkle the rest over the meringues. Bake for 20 minutes; turn the oven down to 110°C (90°C fan oven) mark ¼ and bake for 1¼ hours. Turn off the oven and leave for 30 minutes–1 hour to dry.

2 Sandwich the meringues with the Lemon Filling. Put on a baking sheet and open-freeze until firm. Wrap and refreeze.

3 To serve, transfer the meringue to the refrigerator for 5 minutes. Toast the reserved almonds and sprinkle over the top. Slice, decorate with raspberries and serve with the Raspberry Coulis.

Serves	A LITTLE EFFORT		NUTRITIONAL INFORMATION	
8	**Preparation Time** 30 minutes, plus freezing	**Cooking Time** 1 hour 35 minutes, plus drying	**Per Serving** 420 calories, 24g fat (of which 13g saturates), 49g carbohydrate, 0.1g salt	Vegetarian Gluten free

Nougat Ice Cream

900ml (1½ pints) whole (full-fat) milk
300ml (½ pint) single cream
200g (7oz) white nougat, broken or chopped into chunks
8 medium egg yolks
125g (4oz) golden caster sugar
chopped pistachio nuts and almonds to decorate

1 Pour the milk into a pan and add the cream. Gently bring to the boil. Remove the pan from the heat and add the nougat. Set aside until the nougat has melted, stirring occasionally.

2 Meanwhile, whisk the egg yolks and sugar together in a large bowl. Pour the warm milk and nougat mixture into the bowl, stir well, then pour back into the pan. Cook over a gentle heat, stirring constantly, for about 15 minutes or until the mixture coats the back of a wooden spoon. Pour into a bowl, cool and chill until cold.

3 When cold, tip the mixture into an ice-cream maker and churn according to the manufacturer's instructions until thick. Spoon into a chilled 2 litre (3½ pint) freezerproof container, level the surface and cover with a piece of greaseproof paper. (Alternatively, to make the ice cream by hand, transfer the mixture to the freezerproof container, freeze for 4 hours, then whisk to break up the ice crystals. Freeze for a further 4 hours, then whisk again. Cover with greaseproof paper.) Cover and freeze until ready to serve.

4 Put the ice cream in the refrigerator for 20 minutes before serving to soften slightly. Scoop into balls and scatter with chopped pistachio nuts and almonds.

EASY		NUTRITIONAL INFORMATION		Serves
Preparation Time 20 minutes, plus chilling and freezing	**Cooking Time** 20 minutes	**Per Serving** 520 calories, 32g fat (of which 15g saturates), 48g carbohydrate, 0.5g salt	Vegetarian Gluten free	**6**

Try Something Different

Replace the pistachios with hazelnuts and the dates with dried cherries.

Pistachio and Date Ice Creams

100g (3½oz) shelled pistachio nuts
218g can condensed milk
300ml (½ pint) double cream
1 tbsp orange flower water
125g (4oz) Medjool dates, stoned and roughly chopped
3 pomegranates

1 Keep 15g (½oz) pistachio nuts to one side and put the rest in a food processor. Add the condensed milk and whiz for 1–2 minutes to roughly chop the nuts and flavour the milk.

2 Pour the cream into a bowl and whip until soft peaks form. Stir in the chopped pistachios and condensed milk, orange flower water and dates.

3 Line six 150ml (¼ pint) dariole moulds or clean yogurt pots with clingfilm, leaving some clingfilm hanging over the edges. Spoon in the cream mixture and freeze for at least 5 hours.

4 Cut the pomegranates in half, scoop out the seeds and discard any pith. Push the seeds through a sieve to extract the juice. Put the juice in a pan and bring to the boil, then simmer for 8 minutes until reduced to a syrup. Cool, put in a small airtight container and chill until needed.

5 To serve, ease the ice cream out of the moulds and remove the clingfilm. Cut each in half vertically and arrange on serving plates. Chop the remaining pistachios and sprinkle them over, then drizzle over some pomegranate sauce.

Serves 6	A LITTLE EFFORT		NUTRITIONAL INFORMATION	
	Preparation Time 15 minutes, plus 5 hours freezing		**Per Serving** 516 calories, 38g fat (of which 19g saturates), 38g carbohydrate, 0.4g salt	Vegetarian Gluten free

Spicy Ginger Ice Cream

600ml (1 pint) double cream
125g (4oz) golden caster sugar, plus 1 tbsp
4 medium eggs, separated
2 tsp ground ginger
4 pieces stem ginger, roughly chopped
brandy snaps to serve

For the sauce
50g (2oz) unsalted butter
50g (2oz) golden caster sugar
2 tbsp whisky
2 tbsp ginger syrup (from the jar of stem ginger)

1 Whip the cream until just thick; chill. Whisk 125g (4oz) caster sugar with the egg yolks until pale and creamy.

2 Put the egg whites in a clean, grease-free bowl and whisk until stiff. Beat in 1 tbsp caster sugar.

3 Fold the cream into the egg yolk mixture with the ground ginger, then fold in the egg whites. Pour into a freezerproof container and freeze for 4 hours.

4 To make the sauce, put the butter, sugar, whisky and ginger syrup in a pan and heat gently. Bring to the boil and simmer for 5 minutes or until thick. Cool.

5 Fold the stem ginger through the ice cream and drizzle the sauce over. Stir once or twice to create a ripple effect. Freeze for a further 4 hours or overnight. Serve with brandy snaps.

Serves 8	EASY		NUTRITIONAL INFORMATION	
	Preparation Time 30 minutes, plus 8 hours freezing	**Cooking Time** 5 minutes	**Per Serving** 541 calories, 46g fat (of which 28g saturates), 27g carbohydrate, 0.2g salt	Vegetarian

Try Something Different

Replace the mangoes with 1 small pineapple, and the ratafia with gingernut biscuits.

Mango Ice Cream Terrine

vegetable oil to grease

2 small mangoes, peeled, stoned and chopped

2 medium eggs

125g (4oz) golden caster sugar

300ml (½ pint) double cream, whipped

1½ tsp coconut rum liqueur, such as Malibu

4 ratafia biscuits, roughly crushed

1 Lightly oil a 900g (2lb) loaf tin, then line with clingfilm, leaving some clingfilm hanging over the edges and smoothing any creases.

2 Whiz the mangoes in a food processor or blender until smooth. Set aside. Put the eggs and sugar in a large bowl and whisk together until thick, using an electric hand mixer – this should take 5 minutes.

3 Add the whipped cream to the mixture and fold together with a large metal spoon. Fold in three-quarters of the puréed mango and the coconut liqueur. Spoon the remaining mango purée into the lined tin to cover the base, then pour in the ice cream mixture. Cover with the overhanging clingfilm and freeze overnight or for up to one month.

4 Remove the ice cream from the freezer 5 minutes before serving. Unwrap the clingfilm. Turn out on to a serving dish, sprinkle with the crushed biscuits, slice and serve.

EASY		NUTRITIONAL INFORMATION		Serves
Preparation Time 20–25 minutes, plus overnight freezing		**Per Serving** 306 calories, 21g fat (of which 13g saturates), 26g carbohydrate, 0.1g salt	Vegetarian	**8**

Cinnamon and Nutmeg Ice Cream

½ tsp ground cinnamon, plus extra to dust

½ tsp freshly grated nutmeg

50g (2oz) golden caster sugar

150ml (¼ pint) double cream

250g (9oz) mascarpone cheese

400g carton fresh custard

1 Put the cinnamon, nutmeg, sugar and cream in a small pan, bring slowly to the boil, then put to one side to cool.

2 Put the mascarpone in a large bowl and beat until smooth. Stir in the custard and the cooled spiced cream. Pour the mixture into a shallow freezerproof container and freeze for 2–3 hours.

3 Whisk to break up the ice crystals and freeze for a further 2–3 hours. To serve, scoop into balls and dust with cinnamon.

Serves	EASY		NUTRITIONAL INFORMATION	
8	**Preparation Time** 10 minutes, plus 6 hours freezing	**Cooking Time** 5 minutes	**Per Serving** 221 calories, 15g fat (of which 9g saturates), 16g carbohydrate, 0.1g salt	Vegetarian Gluten free

Cook's Tip

Use any selection of frozen mixed fruit. Summer berries and forest fruits work well.

Frozen Yogurt Sorbet

450g (1lb) frozen mixed fruit, thawed, plus extra to serve
100g (3½oz) clear honey
3 medium egg whites
450g (1lb) low-fat Greek yogurt

1 Line a 750ml (1¼ pint) loaf tin with clingfilm. Whiz the thawed fruit in a food processor or blender to make a purée. Sieve into a bowl, pressing all the juice through with the back of a spoon. Stir the honey into the juice.

2 Put the egg whites in a clean, grease-free bowl and whisk until soft peaks form, then fold into the fruit with the yogurt. Pour the mixture into the lined tin and freeze for 4 hours. Stir to break up the ice crystals, then freeze again for 4 hours. Stir again, then freeze for a further 4 hours or until firm.

3 Put the sorbet in the refrigerator for 20 minutes before serving. Turn out on to a serving plate and remove the clingfilm. Slice and serve with a spoonful of thawed fruit.

EASY	NUTRITIONAL INFORMATION		Serves
Preparation Time 15 minutes, plus about 12 hours freezing	**Per Serving** 120 calories, 6g fat (of which 3g saturates), 14g carbohydrate, 0.2g salt	Vegetarian Gluten free	**8**

Rum and Raisin Ice Cream

250g (9oz) large muscatel or Lexia raisins
100ml (3½fl oz) dark rum
600ml (1 pint) double cream
4 large egg yolks
3 tbsp golden syrup
1 tbsp black treacle

1 Put the raisins in a pan, add the rum and bring to the boil. Turn off the heat and leave to soak while you're making the ice cream.

2 Whip the cream until it just holds its shape. Put the egg yolks, golden syrup and treacle in another bowl. Whisk with an electric hand mixer for 2–3 minutes until it has a mousse-like consistency. Pour into the cream and whisk for 3–4 minutes until thick.

3 Set the freezer to fast-freeze (or turn to coldest setting). Pour the ice cream mixture into a 2 litre (3½ pint) roasting tin and freeze for 45 minutes–1 hour until it begins to harden around the edges.

4 Add the soaked fruit and any remaining liquid to the ice cream and mix well. Put back in the freezer for 45 minutes. Spoon into a 1.7 litre (3 pint) sealable container and freeze for at least 2 hours.

Serves 8	EASY		NUTRITIONAL INFORMATION	
	Preparation Time 40 minutes, plus 3 hours freezing	**Cooking Time** 5 minutes	**Per Serving** 517 calories, 41g fat (of which 25g saturates), 29g carbohydrate, 0.1g salt	Vegetarian Gluten free

Cook's Tip

Sambuca is an anise-flavoured Italian liqueur, whi e Amaretto is almond-flavoured.

Coffee Semifreddi

2 tbsp Sambuca or Amaretto, plus extra to serve

2 tbsp instant espresso coffee, dissolved in 100ml (3½fl oz) water

3 large egg yolks

75g (3oz) caster sugar

300ml (½ pint) double cream, whipped to soft peaks

40g (1½oz) ground almonds, lightly toasted and cooled

1 Line the bases of six 150ml (¼ pint) pudding moulds with greaseproof paper. Stir the Sambuca or Amaretto into the dissolved coffee.

2 In a large bowl, whisk the egg yolks and sugar together until pale and fluffy. Gradually whisk the coffee into the egg mixture.

3 Gently fold in the cream and almonds until all the ingredients are combined. Divide the mixture among the lined moulds and freeze for at least 6 hours.

4 To serve, upturn the moulds on to six serving plates and drizzle a little extra Sambuca or Amaretto around each one. Eat immediately.

EASY	NUTRITIONAL INFORMATION		Serves
Preparation Time 20 minutes, plus 6 hours freezing	**Per Serving** 367 calories, 32g fat (of which 17g saturates), 14g carbohydrate, 0g salt	Vegetarian Gluten free	**6**

Italian Ice Cream Cake

400g (14oz) fresh cherries, pitted and quartered

4 tbsp Amaretto

10 tbsp crème de cacao (chocolate liqueur)

200g (7oz) Savoiardi biscuits or sponge fingers

5 medium egg yolks

150g (5oz) golden caster sugar

450ml (³/₄ pint) double cream, lightly whipped

1 tbsp vanilla extract

75g (3oz) pistachio nuts or hazelnuts, roughly chopped

75g (3oz) plain chocolate, roughly chopped

2–3 tbsp cocoa powder

2–3 tbsp golden icing sugar

1 Put the cherries and Amaretto in a bowl, stir, cover and put to one side. Pour the crème de cacao into a shallow dish. Quickly dip a sponge finger into the liqueur – on one side only, so that it doesn't go soggy and fall apart – then put on to a large chopping board and cut in half lengthways to separate the sugary side from the base. Repeat with each biscuit.

2 Double line a 23cm (9in) round, 4cm (1½in) deep tin with clingfilm. Arrange the sugar-coated sponge finger halves, sugar side down, on the base of the tin. Drizzle with any remaining crème de cacao.

3 Put the egg yolks and caster sugar in a large bowl and whisk until pale and fluffy. Fold in the cream, vanilla extract, nuts, chocolate and cherries, plus any remaining Amaretto. Spoon over the sponge fingers in the tin and cover with the remaining sponge finger halves, cut side down. Cover with clingfilm and freeze for at least 5 hours.

4 To serve, upturn the cake on to a serving plate and remove the clingfilm. Sift cocoa and icing sugar over the cake and leave at room temperature for 20 minutes if the weather is warm, 40 minutes at cool room temperature, or 1 hour in the refrigerator, to allow the cherries to thaw and the ice cream to become moussey. Slice and serve.

A LITTLE EFFORT	NUTRITIONAL INFORMATION		Serves
Preparation Time 40 minutes, plus 5 hours freezing	**Per Serving** 522 calories, 33g fat (of which 15g saturates), 46g carbohydrate, 0.2g salt	Vegetarian	**10**

Try Something Different

For an even more indulgent Christmas dessert, use clotted cream or Bailey's ice cream instead of vanilla.

Cranberry Christmas Bombe

125g (4oz) granulated sugar

300ml (½ pint) cranberry juice

225g (8oz) each cranberries and raspberries, fresh or frozen

2 large egg whites

75g (3oz) caster sugar

groundnut oil to grease

500ml tub vanilla ice cream

For the sugared redcurrants

a few sprigs of redcurrants

1 large egg white, lightly beaten

a little caster sugar

1 Put the granulated sugar and cranberry juice in a pan and heat gently until the sugar dissolves. Bring to the boil, then add the cranberries. Cover and simmer for 15 minutes until very soft. Leave to cool. Blend with the raspberries in a food processor or blender, press through a nylon sieve, then chill. Whisk the egg whites until soft peaks form. Whisk in the caster sugar a spoonful at a time until stiff and glossy. Fold into the fruit purée. Pour into an ice-cream maker and churn until stiff.

2 Meanwhile, lightly oil a 1.4 litre (2½ pint) pudding basin, then put a disc of foil in the base. Put in the freezer for 30 minutes. Spoon the sorbet into the basin, creating a hollow in the centre, and return to the freezer. Leave the ice cream at room temperature for 10 minutes. Spoon the ice cream into the centre of the sorbet and press down well. Freeze for 4 hours or until firm.

3 To make the sugared redcurrants, dip the sprigs in the beaten egg white, then in the sugar. Leave to harden on a baking sheet lined with greaseproof paper.

4 To unmould the bombe, dip the basin in hot water for 10 seconds, then loosen the edges with a round-bladed knife, invert on to a plate, shake firmly and remove the foil. Decorate with redcurrants, then use a warm knife to cut the bombe into wedges.

Serves 8	A LITTLE EFFORT		NUTRITIONAL INFORMATION	
	Preparation Time 30 minutes, plus 6 hours chilling and freezing	**Cooking Time** 15 minutes	**Per Serving** 236 calories, 6g fat (of which 4g saturates), 44g carbohydrate, 0.1g salt	Vegetarian Gluten free

Cook's Tips

Don't over-whip the cream, as the acidity of the raspberries will help to thicken it – aim for a soft dropping consistency.

To make one large soufflé, line the outside of a 1.3 litre (2¼ pint) soufflé dish with a collar of non-stick baking parchment, deep enough to come about 5cm (2in) above the rim of the dish. Omit the chocolate collar (step 2) and don't turn the soufflé out of its dish for serving.

Iced Raspberry Soufflés

juice of 1 orange

juice of 1 lemon

700g (1½lb) raspberries

225g (8oz) caster sugar

450ml (¾ pint) double cream, lightly whipped

2 large egg whites

225g (8oz) plain chocolate

350g (12oz) mixed berries, such as redcurrants, blueberries and blackberries

chocolate curls (see page 21) to decorate

1 Wrap eight 100ml (3½fl oz) glasses with non-stick baking parchment to come 2.5cm (1in) above the glass. Put 2 tbsp each of the citrus juices in a food processor with the raspberries and sugar. Process until smooth, then sieve. Set aside 150ml (¼ pint), cover and chill. Put the remaining sauce in a large bowl, then fold in the cream. Whisk the egg whites until soft peaks form; fold into the raspberry cream. Spoon into the glasses so the mixture reaches the top of the paper. Freeze overnight.

2 Cut eight strips of baking parchment. Melt the chocolate in a heatproof bowl over a pan of gently simmering water. Cool slightly, then brush over the parchment. Remove the soufflés from the freezer and peel off the parchment. Wrap the chocolate-covered strips around the soufflés and freeze for 5 minutes. Peel away the parchment and return to the freezer.

3 Put the soufflés in the refrigerator for 20 minutes before serving. Decorate with mixed berries and chocolate curls and serve with the reserved sauce.

Serves 8	A LITTLE EFFORT	NUTRITIONAL INFORMATION	
	Preparation Time 1¼ hours, plus overnight freezing	**Per Serving** 683 calories, 45g fat (of which 27g saturates), 69g carbohydrate, 0.1g salt	Vegetarian Gluten free

Glossary

Baking blind Pre-baking a pastry case before filling. The pastry case is lined with greaseproof paper and weighted down with dried beans or ceramic baking beans.

Baking powder A raising agent consisting of an acid, usually cream of tartar, and an alkali, such as bicarbonate of soda, which react to produce carbon dioxide. This expands during baking and makes cakes and breads rise.

Beat To incorporate air into an ingredient or mixture by agitating it vigorously with a spoon, fork, whisk or electric mixer. The technique is also used to soften ingredients.

Bind To mix beaten egg or other liquid into a dry mixture to hold it together.

Blanch To immerse food briefly in fast-boiling water to loosen skins, such as peaches or nuts, or to remove bitterness, or to destroy enzymes and preserve the colour, flavour and texture of vegetables (especially prior to freezing).

Brûlée A French term, literally meaning 'burnt', used to refer to a dish with a crisp coating of caramelised sugar.

Candying Method of preserving fruit or peel by impregnating with sugar.

Caramelise To heat sugar or sugar syrup slowly until it is brown in colour; ie forms a caramel.

Chill To cool food in the refrigerator.

Compote Fresh or dried fruit stewed in sugar syrup. Served hot or cold.

Consistency Term used to describe the texture of a mixture, eg firm, dropping or soft.

Coulis A smooth fruit or vegetable purée, thinned if necessary to a pouring consistency.

Cream To beat together fat and sugar until the mixture is pale and fluffy, and resembles whipped cream in texture and colour. The method is used in cakes and puddings that contain a high proportion of fat and require the incorporation of a lot of air.

Crimp To decorate the edge of a pie, tart or shortbread by pinching it at regular intervals to give a fluted effect.

Curdle To cause sauces or creamed mixtures to separate, usually by overheating or over-beating.

Dice To cut food into small cubes.

Dredge To sprinkle food generously with flour, sugar, icing sugar etc.

Dust To sprinkle lightly with flour, cornflour, icing sugar etc.

Extract Concentrated flavouring, which is used in small quantities eg vanilla extract.

Ferment Chemical change deliberately or accidentally brought about by fermenting agents, such as yeast or bacteria Fermentation is utilised for making bread, yogurt, beer and wine.

Folding in Method of combining a whisked or creamed mixture with other ingredients by cutting and folding so that it retains its lightness. A large metal spoon or plastic-bladed spatula is used.

Frosting To coat leaves and flowers with a fine layer of sugar to use as a decoration. Also an American term for icing cakes.

Fry To cook food in hot fat or oil. There are various methods: shallow-frying in a little fat in a shallow pan; deep-frying, where the food is totally immersed in oil; dry-frying, in which fatty foods are cooked in a non-stick pan without extra fat.

Galette Cooked savoury or sweet mixture shaped into a round.

Garnish A decoration, usually edible, which is used to enhance the appearance of a dish.

Glaze A glossy coating given to sweet and savoury dishes to improve their appearance and sometimes flavour. Glazes may be made from beaten egg, egg white, milk or syrup.

Gluten A protein constituent of grains, such as wheat and rye, which develops when the flour is mixed with water to give the dough elasticity.

Griddle A flat, heavy, metal plate used on the hob for cooking scones or for searing savoury ingredients.

Grind To reduce foods such as coffee beans, nuts and whole spices to small particles using a food mill, pestle and mortar, electric grinder or food processor.

Hull To remove the stalk and calyx from soft fruits such as strawberries.

Infuse To immerse flavourings, such as herbs, spices or vanilla, in a liquid to impart flavour. Usually the infused liquid is brought to the boil, then left to stand for a while.

Julienne Fine 'matchstick' strips of citrus zest or vegetables, sometimes used as a decoration or garnish.

Knead To work dough by pummelling with the heel of the hand.

Knock back To knead a yeast dough for a second time after rising, to ensure an even texture.

Macerate To soften and flavour raw or dried foods by soaking in a liquid, eg soaking fruit in alcohol.

Parboil To boil food for part of its cooking time before finishing it by another method.

Pare To finely peel the skin or zest from vegetables or fruit.

Patty tin Tray of cup-shaped moulds for cooking small cakes and deep tartlets. Also called a bun tin.

Poach To cook food gently in liquid at simmering point; the surface should be just trembling.

Prove To leave bread dough to rise (usually for a second time) after shaping.

Purée To pound, sieve or liquidise vegetables, fish or fruit to a smooth pulp. Purées often form the basis for soups and sauces.

Reduce To fast-boil stock or other liquid in an uncovered pan to evaporate water and concentrate the flavour.

Roast To cook food by dry heat in the oven.

Roulade Soufflé or sponge mixture rolled around a savoury or sweet filling.

Roux A mixture of equal quantities of butter (or other fat) and flour cooked together to form the basis of many sauces.

Rubbing in Method of incorporating fat into flour by rubbing between the fingertips, used when a short texture is required. Used for pastry, cakes, scones and biscuits.

Scald To pour boiling water over food to clean it, or loosen skin, eg tomatoes. Also used to describe heating milk to just below boiling point.

Shred To grate cheese or slice vegetables or citrus zest into very fine pieces or strips.

Sieve To press food through a sieve to obtain a smooth texture.

Sift To shake dry ingredients through a sieve to remove lumps.

Simmer To keep a liquid just below boiling point.

Skim To remove froth, scum or fat from the surface of stock, stews, jam etc. Use a skimmer, a spoon or kitchen paper.

Steep To immerse food in warm or cold liquid to soften it, and sometimes to draw out strong flavours.

Stew To cook food, such as fruit and tougher cuts of meat, in a flavoured liquid which is kept at simmering point.

Tepid The term used to describe a temperature of approximately blood heat, ie 37°C (98.7°F).

Vanilla sugar Sugar in which a vanilla pod has been stored to impart its flavour.

Whipping, whisking Beating air rapidly into a mixture with either a manual or electric whisk. Whipping usually refers to cream.

Zest The thin, coloured outer layer of citrus fruit, which can be removed in fine strips with a zester.

Index